DEVOPS, DBAS, AND DBAAS

MANAGING DATA PLATFORMS TO SUPPORT CONTINUOUS INTEGRATION

Michael S. Cuppett

Apress®

DevOps, DBAs, and DBaaS: Managing Data Platforms to Support Continuous Integration

Michael S. Cuppett
Arlington, Tennessee
USA

ISBN-13 (pbk): 978-1-4842-2207-2   ISBN-13 (electronic): 978-1-4842-2208-9
DOI 10.1007/978-1-4842-2208-9

Library of Congress Control Number: 2016960738

Managing Director: Welmoed Spahr
Acquisitions Editor: Robert Hutchinson
Developmental Editor: Laura Berendson
Editorial Board: Steve Anglin, Pramila Balen, Laura Berendson, Aaron Black,
    Louise Corrigan, Jonathan Gennick, Robert Hutchinson, Celestin Suresh John,
    Nikhil Karkal, James Markham, Susan McDermott, Matthew Moodie, Natalie Pao,
    Gwenan Spearing
Coordinating Editor: Rita Fernando
Copy Editor: Nancy Sixsmith
Compositor: SPi Global
Indexer: SPi Global
Cover Image: Designed by Davidzydd / Freepik

Distributed to the book trade worldwide by Springer Science+Business Media New York, 233 Spring Street, 6th Floor, New York, NY 10013. Phone 1-800-SPRINGER, fax (201) 348-4505, e-mail orders-ny@springer-sbm.com, or visit www.springeronline.com. Apress Media, LLC is a California LLC and the sole member (owner) is Springer Science + Business Media Finance Inc (SSBM Finance Inc). SSBM Finance Inc is a Delaware corporation.

For information on translations, please e-mail rights@apress.com, or visit www.apress.com.

Apress and friends of ED books may be purchased in bulk for academic, corporate, or promotional use. eBook versions and licenses are also available for most titles. For more information, reference our Special Bulk Sales–eBook Licensing web page at www.apress.com/bulk-sales.

Any source code or other supplementary materials referenced by the author in this text is available to readers at www.apress.com. For detailed information about how to locate your book's source code, go to www.apress.com/source-code/.

Printed on acid-free paper

Apress Business: The Unbiased Source of Business Information

Apress business books provide essential information and practical advice, each written for practitioners by recognized experts. Busy managers and professionals in all areas of the business world—and at all levels of technical sophistication—look to our books for the actionable ideas and tools they need to solve problems, update and enhance their professional skills, make their work lives easier, and capitalize on opportunity.

Whatever the topic on the business spectrum—entrepreneurship, finance, sales, marketing, management, regulation, information technology, among others—Apress has been praised for providing the objective information and unbiased advice you need to excel in your daily work life. Our authors have no axes to grind; they understand they have one job only—to deliver up-to-date, accurate information simply, concisely, and with deep insight that addresses the real needs of our readers.

It is increasingly hard to find information—whether in the news media, on the Internet, and now all too often in books—that is even-handed and has your best interests at heart. We therefore hope that you enjoy this book, which has been carefully crafted to meet our standards of quality and unbiased coverage.

We are always interested in your feedback or ideas for new titles. Perhaps you'd even like to write a book yourself. Whatever the case, reach out to us at editorial@apress.com and an editor will respond swiftly. Incidentally, at the back of this book, you will find a list of useful related titles. Please visit us at www.apress.com to sign up for newsletters and discounts on future purchases.

The Apress Business Team

I wish to dedicate this book to JoAnn, my wife of 25 years. Thank you for making me a better person, and for doing a fantastic job raising and educating our children.

Your capacity for loving, caring, and encouraging emboldens me to explore opportunities—like authoring a book—far outside of my comfort zone.

Contents

About the Author... ix

About the Technical Reviewer.............................. xi

Acknowledgments xiii

Introduction xv

Chapter 1:   DevOps for DBAs 1

Chapter 2:   DBAs for DevOps 15

Chapter 3:   Integrating DBA and DevOps Processes.............. 25

Chapter 4:   Integrating Database Technologies and DevOps Tools.... 41

Chapter 5:   Stateful Data, Stateless Database Schema, and Code 57

Chapter 6:   Optimizing Application Performance with Change
              Management Improvements...........................73

Chapter 7:   Measuring DBA Inputs to End-User Experience and
              Business Value 87

Chapter 8:   Automation and Code Control 107

Chapter 9:   DBaaS, IaaS, and PaaS............................ 123

Chapter 10:   Overcoming Language and Cultural Barriers
              Between DBAs and DevOps........................ 139

Index 155

About the Author

Michael S. Cuppett is a Business Resiliency Architect for a Fortune 25 healthcare organization, where he currently strives to apply DevOps methodologies to disaster recovery programs. He was previously charged with application and infrastructure reliability, availability, recoverability, and performance as a Solutions Engineer. Cuppett draws on three decades of experience as a DBA and IT engineer in the U.S. Army and the private sector, culminating in a succession of management and senior technology positions at large companies in database administration, solutions engineering, and disaster recovery. Cuppett writes frequent articles on Oracle DBA issues and the business dimension of DevOps for LogicalRead, Oracle Technology Network, and APM Digest. He received a B.S. degree in Management and Computer Information Systems from Park University. Mike lives in Arlington, TN with his wife JoAnn, son John, and daughter Ava.

About the Technical Reviewer

Arup Nanda has been an Oracle DBA since 1993, dealing with everything from modeling to security, and he has a lot of gray hairs to prove it. He has coauthored 5 books, written 500+ published articles, presented 300+ sessions, delivered training sessions in 22 countries, and actively blogs at `arup.blogspot.com`. Nanda is an Oracle ACE Director, a member of Oak Table Network, an editor for SELECT Journal (the IOUG publication), and a member of Board for Exadata SIG. Oracle awarded him the DBA of the Year in 2003 and Architect of the Year in 2012. He lives in Danbury, CT with his wife, Anu and son, Anish.

Acknowledgments

I want to express my sincere appreciation to two extremely supportive and dedicated leaders: Sharyn Lemmons and Gene Weber. Your excitement and reassurance deepened my resolve to complete this project.

Thank you, Arup Nanda, for accepting technical reviewer responsibility to ensure the technical accuracy of the content. Your candid advice made this book better.

To my editors, Robert Hutchinson, Rita Fernando, Laura Berendson, and Matthew Moodie, thank you for offering me this challenging opportunity. I was a first-time book author, and your willingness to guide me through this project sustained my motivation. The Apress process relieved me from having to worry about how to submit or format the manuscript because the clear, step-by-step procedure made managing the work flow simple.

To my many friends with whom I have toiled "in the trenches" for years, know that each of you taught me how to be better at this profession. Thank you for your friendship.

Introduction

DevOps pioneers responded to the need for IT infrastructure and operations (IO) teams to join the Agile movement, a movement guided by principles that focused on delivering business value more quickly; improving customer experience with software products having superior application functionality and stability; and transforming product delivery to iterative, frequent releases to minimize implementation risk. What was initially dubbed *Agile infrastructure* transformed how IO teams deliver services and manage changes: as partners with development. To shore up DevOps teams, DBAs should be invited to the table. DBAs bridge the development and IO gap with application, database, security, audit, infrastructure, and operations experience by offering new capabilities for expanded DevOps coverage.

The intention of this book is twofold: 1) help DBAs understand the DevOps movement cultural shift and what it means to do DevOps from a process perspective and 2) provide insights to DevOps team members of the value DBAs offer and a view into why DBAs diligently protect the database and operations environment from instability and performance challenges. As DBAs assimilate as DevOps team members, the movement advances and benefits customers, businesses, the IT industry, and (most importantly) the professional involved.

I am humbled that Apress recruited me to write this book. This dissertative volume provides perspectives on core deliverables from different angles. If you, the reader, begin to understand the value of adding DBAs to DevOps teams, no matter your current role, it is a win. And if DBAs perceive the cultural dynamic, get excited about transitioning database tasks into the Agile pipeline, start to explore ways to implement the right database for the job (whether on- or off-premise), and understand that the world remains safe even when developers can spin up databases, Apress's vision for this book was realized.

CHAPTER 1

DevOps for DBAs

Organizational demand for agility—adapting the business to meet customer demands and speed—and fulfilling customer demands expediently with an earlier return on investment (ROI) realization continually drive the expanding and maturing cultural paradigm of DevOps. These business-mandated edicts have forced information technology teams, including database administrators (DBAs), to incorporate rapid development, continuous integration, automated testing, and release management. Combined with immediate feedback loops, the result is a shift from monolithic applications to object- or services-defined applications.

This chapter demonstrates how DBA responsibilities are moving from infrastructure builders to infrastructure enablers, from vendor-specific database managers to "best database for the job" proponents; from technology silo experts to technical advisors; from unintentional database metrics isolationists to "metrics for all to see" facilitators; from the "database is green" to the customer experience performance protectors. This disruptive movement looks to adopt more DBAs now that DevOps teams are seeking to strengthen themselves by including DBAs.

To date, DevOps primarily incorporates development (aka programming or software engineering), quality assurance (QA), release management, production operations support, and business team members united in streamlining the software development life cycle (SDLC). Involving DBAs seems to be

© Michael S. Cuppett 2016

M. S. Cuppett, *DevOps, DBAs, and DBaaS*, DOI 10.1007/978-1-4842-2208-9_1

an afterthought; as Pete Pickerill wrote on http://devops.com, "This oversight is unfortunate. DBAs have a lot to offer when it comes to correlating the development of technology with the management of the environment in which it's hosted. In a sense, DBAs have been DevOps all along."[1] It is a costly oversight.

A viable SDLC model no longer consists of sequential, isolated hand-offs from a business analyst to a programmer to a QA tester to a change coordinator, and finally to the last toss over the wall to operations. Instead, each team member performs a *shift left*, shown in Figure 1-1, which describes an earlier involvement in the process, being pulled upstream to learn about business drivers and other reasons why the software being requested is needed, and (perhaps more importantly) learning how the business uses the software.

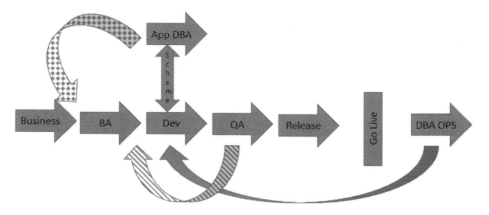

Figure 1-1. Shift-left illustration

QA shifts left to begin building test cases to be used in development and integration; the application DBA shifts left to learn directly from the business what functionality is needed, making the application DBA a more valuable contributor to the solution. The operations DBA, instead of being ill-informed about changes heading toward production, now learns exactly what is in the pipeline, can recommend performance and other operational advice for inclusion in the solution, and can adjust database server templates early in the SDLC.

Teams build better products when each team member understands the purpose for and intended use of the application. When developers hear directly from business team members the features and functionality needed instead

[1]http://devops.com/2015/05/28/where-is-the-dba-in-the-devops-conversation/

of receiving a requirements document with second-hand information translated by a business analyst (BA)—even a very competent BA—the likelihood increases that the software will actually look and perform as requested. In many organizations, BAs are a myth because it is difficult to bridge business language, process, and technical perspective to IT language, process, and technical perspective. Much can be lost in translation, resulting in less efficient use of technology. Whether an application DBA works side by side with the programming team to improve data access code or determine index requirements, or whether an operations DBA toils with release management to ensure the software or service gets moved into production without disrupting the business or degrading application performance, the value-add is clear. Much of this alignment happens by using increased and improved communications, both in person and through specialized tools. DBAs bring tremendous value to the DevOps proposition by contributing deep technical skills and varied experiences that are ready to be leveraged by existing DevOps teams.

Infrastructure Enablers

Database as a Service (DBaaS) empowers anyone—everyone—who needs a database to quickly provision one, without concern for the underlying infrastructure or software installation. Realizing the ease and immediate gratification that DBaaS provides, business and development team members expect DBAs to deliver a near-equal service. Although these teams understand that corporate database provisioning requires proper governance, their delivery expectations are still much sooner than pre-DevOps capabilities. Fortunately, perceived best practices, security requirements, and extended project and purchase approval processes are all realigning to deliver on the promises of DevOps.

DBAs need to exercise judicious discipline, mixed with flexibility and what may feel like overcommunicating, to adapt from silo-ed processes involving receiving hand-offs from an upstream team, sprinkling on a bit of DBA magic, and then passing the package to a downstream team. To work effectively within the DevOps model, DBAs need to manage databases across a variety of platforms: physical or virtual hosts, and internal or external cloud implementations that are likely using database software that is not relational. For DBAs, ensuring secure access and robust access times may be where traditional responsibilities end. New responsibilities include assisting with rapid deployment process (continuous integration and continuous deployment) creation, managing code and scripts using software versioning tools, and building infrastructure as code. Although data remains stateful, the schema, the database software, and the host platform are stateless. DBAs need to become agents of change, supporters of the DevOps methodology, and tactical consultants driven to improve all aspects of the SDLC. DBAs need to become platform and database agnostic. There is more to come on these topics.

Relational databases have been the preferred (best understood) environment for the storage and retrieval of data for several decades. As petabytes of unstructured data have been introduced into the mix, relational databases have struggled to manage the data while staying true to traditional relationship precepts. To fill the gap, NoSQL databases such as Cassandra and MongoDB introduced ecosystems built to store and retrieve data outside of the relational model. (Database specifics are discussed in a later chapter.)

DevOps involves DBAs creating database build templates that developers, yes developers, use to spawn databases on demand, which is simply one step in the automated server provisioning process. Test data loads are automatically consumed, tested, and measured without direct DBA action. DBAs instead help define how the test data is selected and staged for consumption. Learning to accelerate work using automation and source code control for all scripts and code further reduces the development cycle time.

DBAs must aggressively and proactively accelerate product delivery to match the velocity of the release cadence, and be determined to never be the bottleneck.

"Best Database for the Job" Proponents

Particularly for new projects, DBAs need to weigh the impact of force-feeding data into the relational model versus introducing a new database model that is more aligned to the application's expected data use pattern. Structured and unstructured data may best live in separate databases, with applications calling multiple services to read, modify, or delete data. Code is evolving to be more dynamic to leverage multiple back-end databases (see Chapter 5).

Legacy databases will not disappear soon because many still act as the databases of record and contain valuable data. Also, audit and governance requirements have to be satisfied, many by just keeping the data in place until the mandated retention window expires.

Organizations may decide to decouple monolithic application functions into services that fit agile development and DevOps more readily. Segments of data thus may need to be copied or moved into a different database, which is work that DBAs perform regularly. Advantage DBAs: new resume entry!

Technical Advisors

Transforming to align with a business partner's need for scalable, well-performing, and resilient systems, at a lower cost, is much easier when leveraging an established methodology. This methodology has been proven feasible by Netflix, Facebook, Flickr, and Etsy; and DevOps has matured to the point at which even risk-averse organizations should feel comfortable adopting it. Lean processes, obsessive automation, faster time to market, cost reductions, rapid cycle times, controlled failures and recoveries, and robust tool suites empower this ambitious transformation. DevOps DBAs must adapt to this new way of building software products while driving infrastructure stability, resiliency, and availability, eclipsed only by extreme application performance.

DBAs are persistently ostracized for being inflexible, slow to deliver, and generally uncooperative. DBA processes, along with many Operations' processes, remain serialized and burdened by outdated policies and delivery expectations. Shifting to DevOps aligns (absorbs) DBA tasks into combined process flows that began during the agile development transformation. DBAs need to purposefully engage their development peers to communicate a willingness to adopt DevOps practices, manage the infrastructure as code using source control, and learn the implemented tool suite.

DevOps brings many new opportunities for IT teams to deliver superior software products that fulfill business initiatives that lead to excellent customer experiences. On the flip side, challenges arise when integrating processes, increasing release momentum, reducing cycle time, managing infrastructure as code, and implementing change requests. Many DBAs were left behind during the initial DevOps wave; however, current landscape changes include drawing in a variety of IT technicians to further expand capabilities, extend collaboration, reduce waste, and abate SDLC costs.

The inclusion of DBAs into DevOps is not without risk because, as with any process, adding another step, variable, or person increases the possibility for errors or other disruptions. Fortunately, DevOps is supported by ever-evolving powerful tools purposed to assist with collaboration, code management, quality assurance testing, and task automation (some of which are discussed as you progress through this book).

Converting from technology silo experts to technical advisors instills a new sense of purpose and resets our mindset so that we are willing to partner with teams once deemed "nemeses" for the good of the business and the customer.

"Metrics for All to See" Facilitators

DBAs (at least good DBAs) constantly assess the production database environment (code base; database; host operating system [OS]; load; capacity; and, less often, network throughput) and seek opportunities to improve application performance. Whether by identifying poor performing queries, needed indexes, or expanded buffer cache, performance matters to DBAs. The misstep has often been unintentional isolation of performance metrics by not purposefully, holistically, or frequently sharing with network and system administrator (SA), or development team members, although doing so may further improve application performance. More importantly, it provides an exceptional value to customers. Sharing performance metrics enables disparate teams to aggregate their combined experiences and skills, producing opportunities for better solutions than are possible individually. (Chapter 6 delves into a few nondatabase examples of measuring customer experience and how to expand change management to be a DevOps tool for application performance improvement.)

DevOps Success Metrics

Extending metrics beyond customer experience performance management, DevOps introduces measures for software delivery efficiency, release cadence, and success rate. Continuous code integration, automated testing, and continuous delivery have to be measured to determine success. *Continuous integration* checks how well newly introduced code operates with existing code, measured by defects. *Automated testing* checks whether new or modified code function is as defined in the use case and whether the code passes regression testing *Continuous delivery/deployment* checks how often code is released into production (release cadence) and whether the code causes disruption, tracked by incidents.

Customer Experience Performance Protectors

Holistically understanding the infrastructure and application architecture provides opportunities to decrease cumulative degradation, which improves customer experience (see Table 1-1). Even for a basic transaction flow, the delivery level drops rapidly.

Table 1-1. Cumulative Degradation

Cumulative Degradation	
Component	**Success %**
Network	99.9%
Web server	99.7%
App server	98%
Database	97%
App server	98%
Web server	99.7%
Network	99%
Customer Experience:	**91.58%**

Cumulative degradation reveals why the IT five 9's availability goal falls short when measuring customer experience.

Application performance management (APM) can provide transactional perspectives of customer experience, transaction times, and frequency, which provide a framework to fully understand application performance across the infrastructure. DBAs with this transparency level can shift to predictive analysis, allowing corrections to be implemented before the customer notices. Even troubleshooting becomes less problematic and faster because baseline variances can be reported if predetermined thresholds are violated. Additionally, preproduction APM application monitoring can identify code or infrastructure performance deficiencies before release, preventing problems from getting into production.

CAMS

The acronym CAMS[2], originally coined by Damon Edwards and John Willis in 2010, has been used by many authors to describe four essential elements necessary for DevOps success, each in their own words. I intend also to describe these facets within the CAMS framework.

Culture

Internationally recognized management guru Peter Drucker famously pronounced, "Culture eats strategy for breakfast." Culture presents a perplexing challenge to DevOps implementation. Wanting to do DevOps by investing in DevOps tools, training staff, and hiring expert consultants, all without a transferal of mindset, behaviors, and incentives, only suppresses the status quo, which lies quietly below the waves seeking an opportunity to re-emerge.

During a recent client call, a team brought forward a build request for two virtual hosts, including software installs for several products from a popular Agile tool suite. The conversation went something like this:

> Requester: "We need two VMs with tool A and tool B installed for a project starting in 10 days."
>
> SA: "Once approved, it takes 6 weeks to provision a VM."
>
> Requester: "This project has been approved by SVP what's-her-name and VP so-and-so as a fast-track project."
>
> SA: "Our process takes 6 weeks. Then someone still needs to install the tools because that's not what we do."

---

[2]HYPERLINK "http://devops.com/2015/05/28/where

By this time, I am "cryaughing"—trying not to cry or laugh, but really wanting to do both. But I digress.

> Requester: "We are trying to be agile and need to move fast."
>
> SA: "Our process is fast! It used to take 3 months to get a host provisioned."

And so forth. Sadly, this is not a fictional story for book demonstration purposes.

As this unfortunate yet emblematic example shows, existing processes create cultures ingrained with suppositions of how well teams are performing, what people believe are expected from them, and a "don't rock the boat" mindset, all of which present tremendous hurdles to be surmounted. DevOps requires processes to be rethought, leaned out, sped up, and extraordinarily stable. Pulling together strong and patient leaders, complemented by charismatic and uber-respected technical subject matter experts (SMEs) such as DBAs or senior DevOps engineers, to challenge the status quo by instigating a new culture focused on DevOps best practices must be the movement's heart and soul. An organization's culture must transform into a more collaborative, process-defined, and people-centric entity to successfully drive continuous improvement, automation, and integrated testing.

To change the culture, people must at least accept the new direction, even if reluctantly. The best-case scenario includes people being only too happy to scrap the old model and excited to move on to better methods. Both types of people encountered need to be coached differently to effectively ensure the movement's success. The reluctantly accepting group drags its feet, in no hurry to reach the new destination. Coaching increases the pace, improves buy-in, and develops needed attitudes. The excited group (probably the ones who have been telling each other for years that management is a cast of morons and constantly bloviating about how everything would be awesome if only they were in charge) can be more dangerous to the cause than those who may be flat-out resisting the change. Failing to control the ascent with planned and well-communicated phases that include needed staff training, concrete process definitions, and general good change practices may result in a catastrophic crash and burn.

Change is an interesting beast. A team member once asked his manager why the manager had not pushed for a large change that needed to happen. The manager responded that change done gradually over time usually receives better acceptance. The manager's example was for the team member to imagine coming to work the next morning to find a full-grown tree in his cube. The manager explained that even if the employee loved trees, the tree would be bothersome because it had invaded his space unexpectedly. But if the team member arrived to find a potted sapling on his desk, he might think it is cool.

Over time, as he would nurture the sapling (even though he had to repot the now small tree and place it on the floor), the team member would remain comfortable with its presence. After a few years passed, when people would ask him about the full-grown tree in his cube, he would proudly share that he was able to transform a weak sapling into a mighty tree. The employee would accept the change because he was involved (nurturing), and the change came about slowly but consistently.

Driving the new DevOps culture requires introducing a "sapling" and nurturing its growth until the "tree" is well rooted. The more people who are involved in the nurturing process improves the odds of a positive outcome. Leaving the tree-nurturing responsibility in the hands of only the core team likely leads to a brown and wilted sapling.

Automation

It is odd to think that one of the primary benefits unleashed at the dawn of the computer era was the ability to reduce costs and processing time by automating routine tasks. Yet today, when CIOs and their teams are under pressure to drive strategic growth initiatives needed to increase revenue or introduce new products for customers, much of the behind-the-scenes effort is still completed manually. IT professionals (I, too, have been guilty of this) love working with shiny new toys—often at the expense of reducing effort or costs through automation.

DevOps is about speed, flexibility, resiliency, and continuous improvement. People need to understand the processes, build and test the software, implement the automation, and then step back and let the computers do the work. For DBAs, this means relinquishing control of the scripts and surrendering them to source code control. The scripts now become included in the release package instead of being manual executions listed as a task in a plan spreadsheet.

Automation applies to server builds, database software installs and configurations, network settings, storage allocations, schema builds, code compiles, job scheduling, and more. Anything and everything should be automated. Security programs should automatically scan hosts for vulnerabilities. Automation is the way resiliency can be gained, reducing human error risks. The automation itself needs to be monitored and measured to ensure it is delivering expected benefits.

Measurement

People live by measurements. Our day (a measure) is an accumulation of events segmented by the measure of time. The value of our contribution to the organization comes periodically (a rhythm of measures): the amount of our paycheck. Hence, measurements must be important. Yet too many IT shops still focus on binary checks, such as a server being up or down instead of business measures such as end-user experience and transaction capability; or for DevOps: cycle time, failure and resolution rates, release momentum, feature time to market, and reduced SDLC costs.

For DevOps to succeed, a consistent whittling away at inefficiencies, avoidable steps, and pointless multilevel approvals must occur. The burden of CYA and sometimes ego boosting for less-mature executives (e.g., requiring ten people to approve a change) has been known to be one of the most consuming yet valueless requirements related to the SDLC. After all, the business made the request and IT agreed to complete the work, which sounds like approvals. Yes, other oversight is needed, but surely a few approvals would not be missed. Applying lean and Kanban techniques trim inefficiencies that should return value from reduced waste and improved speed. Process mapping, or value stream mapping, should be done to capture the delivery process, see how long each step takes, and evaluate the need for each step. Decisions can then be made to remove impediments, smooth out the workflow, and drop unneeded steps and approvals to produce a streamlined SDLC process.

Sharing

"Knowledge is power." That saying has been around for years, but has been distorted; many people hoard information to be used only for personal gain versus benefiting others. Someone who knows how to cure cancer does not have power by selfishly retaining the solution; instead, the power comes from releasing the information and then watching how the knowledge, when applied, impacts people around the world.

DevOps breathes by sharing information. Business, development, and operations (including DBAs) must communicate in full-duplex. Messages need to be sent and received simultaneously upstream and downstream. Each team member must understand why the business needs the function and how the business plans to use the function. Addressing operational challenges earlier in the process leads to better-performing and resilient production systems. As DevOps expounds continuous testing across the SDLC, all environments must match the planned end-point state. Operational knowledge from team members' vast experience, aggregated into manageable bundles driven upstream to improve the infrastructure, creates consistent and stable platforms.

Do you remember the grade school exercise in which the teacher would share a sentence with one student that was then passed from student to student until the last student relayed the sentence back to the teacher? Whether it was changed intentionally for malice or fun, or changed because students couldn't remember the exact statement, the final message was usually so dissimilar to the original sentence that it was humorous. Unfortunately, this is the exact process IT has used for decades: it receives requirements from the business and then passes the details, which are distorted incrementally, along the supply chain so that (as witnessed far too many times) the business cannot reconcile the final product to the requested functional requirements.

DevOps must have a continuous feedback mechanism that constantly relays information concerning code and infrastructure decisions that seamlessly apply to production, and which decisions disrupt or degrade the customer experience by degrading application performance or availability.

Figure 1-2 shows a continuous loopback system underlying the code-progression process.

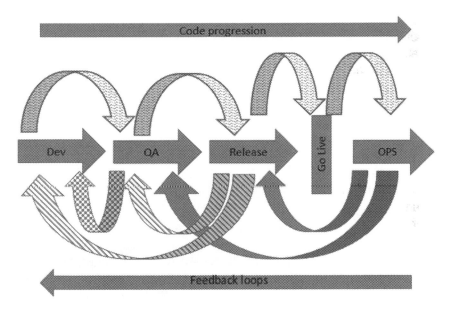

Figure 1-2. Feedback loops

Thinking Differently

Earlier involvement in the SDLC introduces challenges, maybe even opposition, to traditional responsibilities. Customary DBA tasks seem often to be outliers concerning the SDLC. Although analysis, development, QA testing, releases, and initial operations support efforts stream as a continuous flow, DBA tasks have a tendency to abruptly change the flow, disrupting progress. As DevOps database frameworks mature, DBA task inclusion becomes seamless to the process, supporting continuous integration and automation.

Core DBA work shifts from being a significant Gantt chart bar to barely a blip on the timeline. Imagine not being constantly asked, "When will the database be ready?"; instead not even being a part of the build and release cycle. How? Infrastructure as code, which involves predefining database configurations that can be built on virtual resources, initiated by developers on demand. Also shifting to DevOps, SAs can purchase, rack and stack, power up, and network attach computing resources as an internal cloud, ready for consumption. Optionally, provisioning platforms may simply mean consuming external cloud resources (an example is DBaaS). Either way, SAs can create templates for standard server builds: database, app server, web server, and so on. DBAs can then extend the database server build templates to include database software installation and database creation. Including test data loads for preproduction databases for testing can also be automated. All scripts used in the build process must be managed as code, including versioning and source code control. DBAs need to manage their code just like their development partners.

Security, everyone's concern, has at least three tasks: 1) scan and approve template-driven server builds; 2) dictate access methods and privileges for the operating system, database, web services, and more; and 3) periodically scan active servers for vulnerabilities. DBAs must provide continual feedback to the security team to ensure risk mitigation.

With this automation, the SDLC pipeline no longer includes long duration bars for purchasing and building servers and databases; instead, developers can provision on demand. Yes, the hairs on my neck are standing up, too. Remember that although you still control the installation, build, and configuration of the database, you can turn your focus to performance and customer experience improvements once you have automated provisioning.

Now that servers are provisioned from predefined templates with or without using a DevOps tool, platform consistency begins to evolve. As code progresses toward production, needed environments are spun up using the same template as the initial development server. In some cases, even the production ecosystem is built exactly like every server involved in the code release process. Appreciating that production web and app server builds from templates can be a successful model is one thing, but accepting that idea for production database servers needs more consideration. Agreeing that only data is stateful allows the inference that the data could be loaded and unloaded, even transformed to meet business requirements. Consequentially, it is unlikely that a multiterabyte relational database would undergo that much manipulation. In these cases, DBAs may choose to derive the preproduction database configuration from the production setup, maintaining platform consistency. Mike Fal writes in the simple talk blog posting, *DevOps and the DBA*, "The reality is that chaos, instability, and downtime are not the result of speed, but the result of variance."[3]

---

[3]-is-the-dba-in-the-devops-conversation/" http://devops.com/2015/05/28/wh

Inconsistencies between nonproduction and production environments have always undermined production releases (it worked in development), extended outages (change ABC implemented 2 months ago was never removed from production, which caused this release to fail), and degraded performance (it was fast in QA) because the solution could not scale to the production load.

Marching forward, DBAs have the opportunity to improve platform stability, remove build bottlenecks, and increase production resiliency by collaborating toward on–demand provisioning capabilities, reducing failures caused by inconsistency, and most importantly, being cultural change warriors. Many of you are already doing DevOps work—now there is a name to help facilitate conversations.

Summary

DevOps presents exciting opportunities for DBAs to make the improvements that many of you have wanted for years. As the culture shifts to align with the agile and DevOps movements, and DevOps teams understand the valuable contribution that DBAs bring to DevOps, DBAs can more directly influence application performance and infrastructure stability while being able to provide better–fitting database solutions with the incorporation of NoSQL environments and DBaaS offerings.

DBAs need to become automation experts to create and maintain database build templates, integrate with server build templates, and let others do the actual builds. They check in database change code for absorption into the continuous integration pipeline, build numerous tests to expose all possible defects to prevent them from progressing toward product delivery, and intend to never allow a defect to be deployed into production.

The following chapters expose DBAs to DevOps, provide insights into "why" and "how" to do DevOps; discuss the value proposition; and present easily explainable examples of platform usage, database selection, and points where DBA can be inserted in the pipeline. No programming experience is needed to understand the stateful and stateless code examples.

Welcome DBAs to DevOps!

DBAs for DevOps

Experienced DevOps professionals have the responsibility to assimilate new people into the movement. DBAs coming on board need to understand (and possibly be convinced) that DevOps is about improving and quickening a continuous flow of software or web service improvements designed to provide a richer customer experience, abounding with excellent performance and extreme availability. DBAs need to change many habits to blend traditional work into the DevOps model.

DBA "Undersight"

DBA work has been a "black box" for too long. In Chapter 1, I mentioned "magic" as a DBA tool. I was joking, of course, but reality shows that DBA scripts, database performance configuration changes, login triggers, and other DBA outputs are not scrutinized enough nor managed properly. The change advisory board (CAB) team may ask a question or two about why the change is needed, but many CAB members probably do not have the required knowledge to question the change enough to understand the potential harm. I hear what you are thinking, "The CAB does not have the technical experience to interrogate most changes." I agree, but I also maintain the position that the CAB members see fewer database changes (compared with application changes) and fail to realize that database change mistakes tend to lean toward catastrophic. I believe it's because the CAB should not be evaluating changes. The product

© Michael S. Cuppett 2016
M. S. Cuppett, *DevOps, DBAs, and DBaaS*, DOI 10.1007/978-1-4842-2208-9_2

owner and DevOps team members should know when to deploy because they intimately know the readiness of the code, understand the consequences of failure, and are working the backlog based on value. DevOps protects the teams from consequences if the teams abide by the mandates to excessively test to code and never allow a defect to be deployed into production. DBAs and DevOps team members surely agree to this value proposition, not needing oversight for releases. You'll have to persistently engage the DBAs to shift expectations in order to incorporate their work into the release cycle.

"Bridg-ers"

Although DBAs fortunately have the rare ability to bridge the gap between development and operations, they have been detrimentally overlooked in many companies that deploy DevOps practices. A DBA's ability to interrogate code and construct a resilient, well–performing database environment uniquely defines the capabilities needed for DevOps. DevOps requires transformation from organizational silos defined by a technology skill set to process-driven, continuous flowing work streams that are empowered by collaboration and automation. DevOps is about speed, delivery time, continuous integration and deployment, release cadence, and superior customer experience. Although metrics are critical for measuring customer experiences such as application responsiveness, they are also needed to measure release success rate, software defects, test data problems, work, and more.

DBAs tend to be strong technical leaders who provide insight into coding best practices, host platform configurations, database performance improvements, data security and protection. To be successful, DBAs have to communicate, collaborate, teach, and learn while continuously improving database performance and availability. The job often includes having to meet with development to discuss poor performing code, index requirements, or execution plans to recommend code remediation. These "normal" interactions are imperative to the success of DevOps, leaving me perplexed about why DBAs were not one of the first operations team members asked to join the DevOps movement.

Transition

Understanding that DBAs are "built" in significantly different ways should help with the approach. Many DBAs were once developers, others came from various infrastructure roles, and still others have always been DBAs. Determining which DBA type is easier to bring into the fold is a fool's game. DBAs are people, and people are surprisingly unpredictable. One ex-developer DBA may be excited to finally be able to use both skill sets to help advance DevOps, whereas another may be perturbed by having to dig up old skills she had hoped were long dead and buried. Individually interviewing and evaluating each DBA may be necessary. Much like interviewing potential employees, discernment is needed to assess fit, training needs, and potential disruptive factors that may impact the existing DevOps team members. As mentioned in Chapter 1, the right leaders and SMEs need to be involved and dedicated to the time and effort needed to integrate DBAs. Rest easy; the good news is that even if some DBAs may resist, they all want to provide value by improving the environment.

Besides, as you start to expand participation in DevOps, you already have a handful of people in mind to make the voyage smoother. You know who I'm talking about. Yes, the ones you see talking to the development teams on a regular basis, checking in to see how things are going, seeing what changes are coming down the pipe, asking what the application users are saying about performance, and even offering to assist as needed. These people should be your initial picks to join the DevOps team. Specifically, you should find DBAs who are already engaged, bring them on board, and then let them help you select and onboard other DBAs when needed.

Having a trusted and respected DBA doing the team's bidding for additional DBA talent is likely to result in volunteers. People want to work with people with whom they have an established relationship. Leverage previous successful working relationships to resourcefully construct the DevOps team.

Reciprocal Teaching

Whether through formal methods such as classroom or virtual training, job shadowing, and mentoring; or through informal methods such as team discussions or presentations, teaching needs to be a frequent element of team integration. It is a given that IT and business teams have difficulty understanding each other without a common taxonomy. Even teams within IT often fail to understand each other. A developer discussing encapsulation or inheritance may totally perplex a DBA unfamiliar with object-oriented programming terminology. Never mind if you start talking about Agile, which is very new to many IT professionals. Likewise, a DBA ranting about developers "thrashing" the buffer cache is likely to see the "deer in the headlights" stare. While investigating a performance issue specific to a screen, a developer shared with a DBA that the drop-down window would display ten data elements from which the application user could select. As they looked at the code and then tested the code in a nonprod environment, they learned that the result set was millions of records. The million records would move from the database to the middle tier, and then the needed to rows would be pushed to the client application screen. When asking why millions of rows were being returned, the developer said that was a standard practice. After looking into other queries, the DBA soon found herself ranting to several development managers about the developers thrashing the buffer cache and the performance impact. After realizing that these managers did not understand DBA "technical" jargon, she determined that there was a better way to communicate the message. She scheduled a meeting a few days later, in which she put together a presentation deck outlining basic buffer cache concepts with visuals (see Figure 2-1) that demonstrated how large result sets can negatively impact not only the query requesting the data but also every aspect of the database performance.

Blocks being read into the buffer cache will consume empty blocks first, but will then force "inactive" blocks to be flushed from the cache to complete the read. Then, if the query that had read in the flushed blocks needs those blocks, the blocks will be re-read back into the cache. This process of flushing and re-reading blocks repeatedly is called "thrashing the buffer cache". DBAs and developers must work together to prevent this performance problem.	Empty, accepts new read block	Empty, accepts new read block	Empty, accepts new read block	Empty, accepts new read block	Empty, accepts new read block
	Empty, Accepts read block	Empty, accepts new read block	Empty, accepts new read block	Empty, accepts new read block	Empty, accepts new read block
	Flushed, accepts new read block	Flushed, accepts new read block	Flushed, accepts new read block	Flushed, accepts new read block	Flushed, accepts new read block
	No change, data from earlier read	No change, data from earlier read	No change, data from earlier read	No change, data from earlier read	No change, data from earlier read
	No change, data from earlier read	No change, data from earlier read	No change, data from earlier read	No change, data from earlier read	No change, data from earlier read

Figure 2-1. Buffer cache thrashing

After the DBA spent an hour walking the developers through the presentation and answering questions, these developers understood the impact of less-selective queries. As days and weeks passed, and often when the DBA was visiting the developer realm, developers would jokingly remind each other to not thrash that buffer cache unless they wanted the DBA to get after them. Although the training was succinct and simplified, it closed the language gap, resulting in improved query selection criteria, smaller result sets, and less buffer cache "thrashing." The point is that even people in the same industry do not necessarily speak the same language. DevOps introduces another language gap that requires purposeful definition to keep all members of the team aligned. This book presumes that readers are technically savvy and already familiar with DevOps and the core terminology, but it may not be true as they begin working with DBAs. Accelerating DBA engagement requires DBAs to understand the DevOps principles and foundational constructs.

Experienced DevOps team members need to educate DBAs on processes, continuous integration and delivery, and the implemented tool set. Demonstrating how code is built, tested, integrated, and released helps DBAs determine where best to interject changes supporting the code cycle. DBAs also need early notification when system changes are necessary, allowing time for the reconfiguration to be completed, tested, security approved, and automated for pipeline consumption.

Processes Anew

Differentiating which DBA inputs to put forth for absorption into existing agile and DevOps processes demands collaborative effort between existing team members and newly assigned DBAs. Cohesive integration to advance the undertaking of capturing additional value at decreased costs lengthens the backbone—the code generation process definitions from start to finish—of the movement, triggering existing processes to be rehashed, or repurposed, and then reacclimated within the SDLC cycle.

Together, DBAs and DevOps team members make old things new again as processes throughout the development, testing, release, and operations support pathway are refined to incorporate DBA tools, change methods, and metrics. The critical goal is to not disrupt the code delivery schedule while reaffirming the automation and process sequence preciseness. Sanctioning a parallel environment that initially mirrors the primary build-to-release architecture onto which the DBA components get added enables a side-by-side comparison to ensure that updated processes work correctly. Of course, automation oversees the execution, examination, and effects reporting.

Quick to Value, Delight the Customer

Excitement for DevOps, besides the "it's the cool thing now" factor, stems from years of frustration as IT professionals have been viewed as money-wasting, unresponsive, slow to deliver, and second-rate business citizens. One of my pet peeves has been the "IT alignment to the business" language. Viewing IT as an "outside" entity having to blend in plans to support or conform to the rest of the business accounts for much disillusion and poor *esprit de corps*.

When agile development (and DevOps in close pursuit) exploded in popularity, IT folks finally envisioned a promising future in which product delivery proficiencies incessantly eliminate time, process, approval, and implementation waste, and then rocket delivery to the customer. One Lean principle is *establish pull*. Customers establish pull inherently when reporting problems or requesting new product functionality. IT's capability to deliver has never been this radically empowered, in which demand (pull) can be satisfied within a customer's time expectations.

As consolidated teams, call them agile or DevOps, build new or decouple established services from monolithic applications, change footprints become much smaller (think microservices), making it possible to deploy code quickly with minimal risk. With speed united with smaller code chunks, a failed release becomes no more than a temporary blip on the radar.

Fail Forward, Fail Fast

Application programming interfaces (APIs), microservices, web services, and objects have all been "invented" to eliminate complexity, unreadability, tremendous testing requirements, and massive release risk associated with applications containing thousands, hundreds of thousands, or more lines of code. Even "package" applications can require multiple objects (packages) to be modified for a single functional change. Each touch point increases risk. Dissecting large code segments into services, for example, decreases the time needed to find the code to be modified, which reduces testing time. With DevOps, the duration is decreased further by using automated testing and minimizes the potential release impact on the production environment.

Compiling, packaging, and deploying large applications at once into production are some of the major reasons for disgruntlement between development and operations. The release causes huge problems for the business and customers, with operations under the gun to find and rectify the failure—often with no development assistance. That division ends with DevOps. Now that development and operations work together during the coding, testing, release, and production support phases, true partnerships develop that provide significant business value and team harmony.

Services mimic real-life situations, increasing focus. Here's a bank analogy: when you step up to the teller to make a deposit, you expect a quick and problem-free transaction to occur. Really, you care about little else. The teller does not need to know how you got the money, where you came from, or how you got to the bank (whether you drove or had someone drive you). This information doesn't matter for the transaction to be completed. For you, knowing how the bank checks to make sure you are a customer with an active account, how the money flows from the teller to the safe, how the transaction is audited internally, or which bank industry best practice for deposit transactions are being applied means little. You simply want to hand the teller your cash and/or checks and a deposit slip, and receive a receipt verifying the deposit into your account. Managing code as services or APIs, for example, supports real-life conditions by reducing code to the smallest number of lines or functions needed to carry out its purpose.

Code that expects and accepts only a few "requests," which then performs one or two discrete actions and finally returns the "response," makes it possible to accept the "fail fast, fail forward" model. Being able to deploy distinct code elements quickly, matched with the ability to deploy the next release version or the previous version, facilitates moving forward, even on failure. The small program unit minimizes the production impact upon failure—maybe only a few people experience the problem instead of a large set of application users when large code deployments go wrong. Instead of backing out a massive change because it would take too long to find the root cause for the failure, the small footprint can be overlaid quickly, rectifying the problem while potentially advancing the code. This model makes sense, although years of "backing out" have incorrectly indoctrinated our perception. Think about it; have you even fallen backward when you trip while walking or running? No, most likely you recover without falling, or momentum keeps you moving forward even if you do fall. DevOps leverages momentum to maintain forward progression. Remember, though, failing forward cuts across the grain for DBAs who are used to protecting operational stability at all costs, making not rolling back failures a seemingly unnatural act. Experiencing only frequent successful fail forwards brings DBAs fully onboard.

Continuous Integration, Continuous Testing

Besides implementing small code segments, there are two additional reasons why fail forward has proven successful: continuous integration and testing. For DBAs whom you mentor, that means shifting direction from isolated inlands of specific tasks to inclusion directly into the code-producing effort. Code, schema changes, and even job scheduling tasks have to assimilate into the software code process, including the way DBA code is built, tested, version controlled, and packaged for release. In Chapter 1, you learned that server clones, each built from the same script, eliminate platform variability, making application systems more resilient. For this reason, all software has to be managed without variability from start to finish. The only exceptions are new or modified code requested by the business or customers.

The continuous flow of code into production may initially disorient DBAs because the release and postrelease support model has been a brutalizing cultural norm for decades. It is patterned like this: deployment night = pull an all-nighter and then get a little sleep before being called back into the office because the business is about to implode on itself (a total distortion of reality) if the problem is not fixed promptly. After hours of troubleshooting, someone discovers that the C++ library was not updated on the production system, causing updated code to run incorrectly with the older library files. In this case, the production system obviously was a huge variable, requiring separate work to upgrade the compiler that was missed as the release progressed. Variability burns you nearly every time.

Repeating from Chapter 1: when the production system has to remain, the best move is to clone the nonprod environments from the production server. Once the first nonprod server is built, the process can be automated to manage additional server builds. When something like an upgrade to the C++ libraries is needed, test for backward compatibility; if successful, upgrade production, clone production, and start the nonprod builds. When older code fails (perhaps due to deprecated commands or libraries) and forces the upgrade to be included in a larger release of all code needing to be modified for the new libraries, very stringent change management processes must be adhered to. This scenario is becoming more rare because agile development and database management tools have been built to overcome these legacy challenges.

Tools of the Trade

Agile development and DevOps have not only changed how code is built, tested, released, and supported, and changed how teams collaborate to be successful, but new suites of tools were also specifically built to transform the SDLC. There is a movement away from waterfall project management—serialized code progression starting with development and then proceeding to testing, integration, quality assurance, and production.

New opportunities to create applications in weeks or even days has led to products being produced and then held for release until the company can be officially formed and readied for business operations. That reality did not seem possible a short 10 years ago. Powerful tools have enabled businesses to move from "scrape together a little money, spend most of the money forming the company, start coding, go hungry, sleep in the car, beg for more money from family and friends, visit Mom and Dad to get laundry done and consume real food, and release version 1 in desperation, hoping to generate enough revenue to fix numerous bugs to be released as version 2" to an early-capture revenue model in which the application is built and readied to release and generate revenue, possibly even while the paperwork to form the company is underway. Imagine releasing an application on the day the company comes into existence, possibly even recognizing revenue on day 1. Today, if the product is conservatively successful, the continuously growing revenue stream allows focus toward new products instead of figuring out where the next meal comes from. Tools empower possibilities.

Best time ever for software startups!

Years of experience looking at performance metrics, CPU, memory and disk space utilization, hit ratios, and SQL execution times translates easily into other tool sets. Even process building, test automation, regression, and release automation tool sets fail to challenge any but the most-junior DBAs. Working with tools comes easily for DBAs. Logically developing process flows to incorporate database administrative tasks accelerates the SDLC. The biggest challenge may be selecting which tools are needed from among the plethora of popular DevOps tools.

As DBAs progress through the stages necessary to transition, become educated and share knowledge, learn that small failures are a part of the plan, morph their tasks into the mainstream workflow, and become tool experts, DevOps teams become stronger by sharing experiences, technical skills, improved collaboration, and (most importantly) trust.

Molding DBAs

Adding DBAs to DevOps teams gives the DevOps team members the opportunity to "mold" the DBAs. Previous challenges of getting a DBA to even consider a nonrelational database solution becomes an opportunity for the DBA to learn new database technologies. Just climbing over the fence gives new perspective. Once DBAs buy into DevOps, learn the processes, and fully understand how database work can benefit the business, instead of the development team (the previous customer), the pipeline expands from database change introduction, growing the code base as DBAs check in database changes and infrastructure as code templates and scripts. Cycle time shrinks from database changes no longer being an outlier to the process. Deployments smooth out and complete faster as DBA work is automated.

DBA Value Proposition

DBA participation in DevOps draws in a critical application availability and performance contributor: the database. Involving DBAs means that application code is evaluated from a different perspective, especially calls to the database. Database changes become integrated code for continuous integration and exhaustive testing. DBAs can identify poorly executing queries and transactions and baseline production performance. They can get ahead of forthcoming code changes or new functionality by understanding the impact on the preprod environments, which gives DBAs time to analyze and implement performance-tuning enhancements before the additional load is present.

Problems become challenges for a larger team, compiling more experiences and skills into the pool of contributors to determine root cause and deploy mitigation. DBAs' experiences in other infrastructure areas add another layer of value by being able to assess the application and database by looking under the covers at the operating systems, storage, and network. Further discussion is ahead.

Closer and constant DBA and DevOps team collaboration improves product outcomes, stability, security, and performance, which lead to happier customers and improved business results. As DBAs better understand the business team's use of the product, building a disaster recovery solution or recovery from backup strategy can be customized

Giving developers the freedom to fire up virtual hosts with different database options enables consideration of risk early in the process. A developer wanting to test a new data access service can test, retry, and destroy the virtual host to start over with a fresh host if necessary. DBAs scripting different template options applicable to different data platforms shifts experimentation from production too early in the pipeline.

Summary

DBAs are a good match for DevOps. Driven to improve performance, reliability, and system stability; and matched with the skills to adapt, analyze, and execute process improvements, DBAs can expand the DevOps team's capabilities; reduce cycle time by pulling database changes into the continuous integration process; contribute new test cases for improved bug detection; and get ahead of performance, load, and other operational challenges before production impact.

By investing in DBAs joining DevOps teams, DevOps leaders and engineers increase influence and impact on the business. Applying proven DevOps processes to database changes, build templates, database selections, and broader platform considerations presents new opportunities that may have been previously resisted by the same DBAs. DBAs get excited when their contribution can grow, they can grow, and the business can grow.

Integrating DBA and DevOps Processes

Shifting the culture and aligning team members mark progress toward shortening the virtual to-do list for bringing DBAs into the DevOps fold. Early stage buy-in for DBAs and existing DevOps staff may not be a full commitment, and constructing the process integration methodology becomes key to completing the transformation to the desired future state. Months, even years, of planning, investing, growing, battling, losing, and winning committed to Agile development now comes face to face with the biggest threat: more people and more work. Expanding to include the delivery of database changes into and through the pipeline introduces risk, risk creates anxiety, and anxiety causes apprehensiveness, which may lead to aloofness. However, seasoned Agile developers have learned from an agile prime directive—change is welcomed.

As a DBA, you will start hearing some odd terminology: branches and trunk, recipes, cookbooks, sprints, iterations, backlogs, Kanban, product owners, extreme programming, value streaming, and more, depending on the mix of Agile and DevOps tools, and the project methodologies established within your organization. This book, along with Google, Bing, and vendor product web sites, should be a go-to resource for the duration of your learning curve.

© Michael S. Cuppett 2016
M. S. Cuppett, *DevOps, DBAs, and DBaaS*, DOI 10.1007/978-1-4842-2208-9_3

Disruptors (in this case, the DBAs) realize that being tasked to drive further development and overall IT costs down, increase release frequency, and reduce production problems by implanting automated database changes into a refined process built by others demands finesse. In principle, most people agree that the logical evolution beyond agile development is DevOps; database changes and DBAs are a single representation from many infrastructure and operations elements, albeit the potentially most intrusive and destructive force. Figure 3-1 speaks volumes, showing why database changes hold court more often than other I/O functions.

Figure 3-1. Big bang release driven by code changes needing to match database changes

Whether this scenario occurs in nonproduction or production environments, the results are disruptive more times than not. What used to be a series of software releases mixed with large, risky application and database big bang releases (see Figure 3-2) morphs into a smoother, risk-minimizing pipeline (see Figure 3-3).

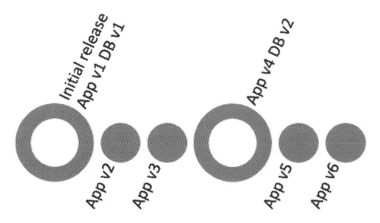

Figure 3-2. Disruptive release adding risk to agile pipeline

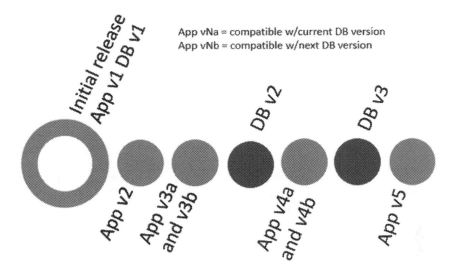

Figure 3-3. Cohesive pipeline minus large risk DB/App releases; application gets toggled

Implementing code that can be toggled to activate or revert versions matched with well-planned deployment scheduling allows for much smoother and less-complicated application and database releases. Code adaptations for multiple schema versions lessen release disruption. Let's use different SQL statements based on code version to describe a simple application toggling example. As shown in Figure 3-3, code versions 3a and 3b are implemented together, with version 3a as the active code. When the database change is implemented, the code version, a metadata update, has to be toggled to version 3b. Here's how the events play out:

Normal application work by users

Release 1

- Deploy code versions 3a and 3b
- Update mymetadatatable to set application version at 3a

Normal application work by users

Release 2

- Deploy schema change that adds a column to a table
- Update mymetadatatable to set application version to 3b

Normal application work by users

As for the code difference, the SQL statement in version 3a does not include the new column, which the SQL statement in version 3b does include. Prior to SQL statement execution, a simple query is made to the mymetadatatable to get the current application version followed by an IF statement that chooses the path matching the code version.

Release 1 was an application change, and release 2 was a database change, done with code toggling to simplify the process. In the days before DevOps, it would have been one release, including the application and database changes and many more code and database changes, introducing significant change-driven risk.

DevOps changes the game by working to implement the smallest change possible to minimize risk. There may be 1,000 changes per day, but each is miniscule and easy to roll back or forward with the next version. Containerization is a perfect example of "containing" changes to the smallest possible footprint because a container can be built and destroyed with very little impact on the user experience.

Although not every database change can be absorbed this way, past practices of piling up database changes should be demolished, just as the walls between development, infrastructure, and operations are demolished by DevOps. Complexity is the nemesis of smart people. Simplicity empowers smart people working collaboratively toward common goals and incentives to better control risk while completing more deployments at smaller intervals, and getting enhancements to the customer more quickly, which meets business demand better than monthly or quarterly releases.

Code Handling Pre- and Postdatabase Change

Database changes have always been part of the software development lifecycle for applications that need to store and retrieve information. Being incorporated formally into the agile environment expansion (DevOps), database change release timing now needs to be more precise. Under waterfall, database changes and application changes tended to be two different threads running in parallel, with the DBAs planning a release and potential outage prior to or in conjunction with the software product release dependent on the database change. Risks escalate from the dependency and larger implementation. Even if the dual release may have occurred in several nonproduction environments, production is where many unnoticed or unfound complications like to reveal themselves.

Pulling database changes onto the application thread, singularizing the release flow, allows small iterative releases to continue, mitigating the risk with flexible code adaptations. Building code that works for both the prerelease and postrelease database versions mitigates the all-in release risk.

Notice that prior to each database change, the code has been constructed to function with or without the database change, making it possible to abstract the software release from the database release—the dependency driving the larger, riskier release has been remediated.

The search function in Microsoft Excel does not require modification as the column and row counts increase or decrease, or when a column data type changes. The search function reads all the data, looking only for required matches and ignoring the rest of the data. Similarly, building code that is agnostic or adaptive to database changes minimizes release size risk. For example, NoSQL database tables, called *documents*, do not have declarations for the data types stored in the document, whereas tables in a relational database require the columns to be defined before data can be inserted. When inserting data into a relational database table, the programmer must order the data by column sequence or explicitly name each column; for a document, the sequence is not important. For example, XML files have been around for some time, so data contained in an XML file has a tag that identifies the data, making the order inconsequential.

DBAs and developers work together to sequence releases and build test cases designed to discover potential code failure specific to the database modification, flushing out problems prior to production. DBAs with programming skills may even be able to produce the code needed to interact with the database changes, alleviating developer load while tightening team bonds.

Release Considerations

Agile development code automation starts at the source code repository, whether the continuous integration server is triggered by each code commit or scheduled for a daily run to consume new or modified code branches into the main trunk through to deployment. Although the work may be fully automated, the sequence might include deliberate stops. For instance, a company that produces software for other companies probably wants to ensure that the software product is always deliverable—fully tested and ready for deployment. But because the company has to be able to support released versions, software releases to customers are balanced between being able to deliver customer requested or needed functionality with the company's capability to support all released product versions. Even this control is subsiding because mobile applications update frequently, sometimes without notification. Understanding DevOps processes makes you aware that mobile apps are not likely to roll back and impact thousands or even millions of people. Instead, a fix gets developed and deployed quickly to roll over the problematic version.

Organizations that build software for internal consumption can remain flexible in release planning. Enhancements to the corporate informational web site can be fully automated through deployment because the risk from content updates is minimal and they can be quickly corrected. In contrast, a major rewrite of the company's market differentiating application has significant downside considerations. Additional internal testing, key customer testing, and dark or canary release management may be necessary to prove application readiness.

Canary Releases

Canary releases are based on the dated and unreliable use of canaries in coal mines to prevent asphyxiation. The premise was that the canary falling over dead from dissipated oxygen levels served as a warning for the miners to vacate the mine. Unlike alpha or beta releases, canary releases occur in production using production-ready code that is managed to impact a small group of customers.

A software canary release is simply a purposeful implementation strategy to limit the number of customers using and being potentially impacted by the new release. As Figure 3-4 shows, the new software is released onto only one of the four application servers in the load balanced pool. Whether a fourth server is added to an existing three servers or an existing server was repurposed matters not. Configured as shown, only 10% of the company's customers are testing the new product version, thereby not risking upsetting the entire customer base. If complaints hit the help desk specific to the new software product, the one application node can quickly be removed from the load balanced pool, making the new software unavailable. If the new product proves to be a success with the small group of customers, implementation can proceed slowly (a node can be updated each day until fully deployed) or the product can be deployed as quickly as possible to every application server. There are plenty of options.

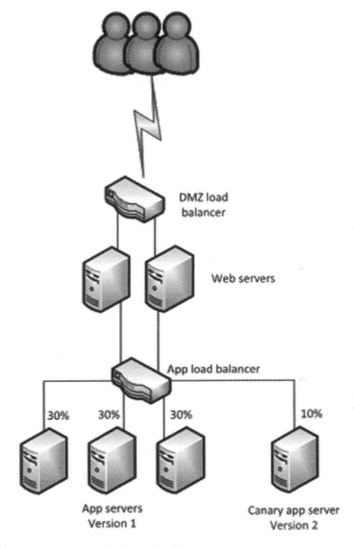

Figure 3-4. A canary server with limited traffic

As shown in Figure 3-4, rolling implementations obviously become an option. Having the agility to keep operations running while deploying software is a paradigm shift for many corporations. Large releases during dark windows when the application environment is unavailable are quickly becoming an unacceptable practice, especially for global participators. Imagine Amazon or Netflix shutting down once a month for a code release; it is unthinkable!

Rolling Upgrades

In a load-balanced, ten-node application server example, a rolling deployment would consist of removing one node from the load balancer (certain load balancers can support automated node management), applying the new code to the defected node, and then returning the node into the available pool. The process then repeats until all the nodes are running the new code, which completes the release. Having 90% of the application capacity online during the release should serve the customer base without notice, except maybe during peak loads. For peak load implementations, the online capacity could be expanded beyond 100% before rolling the upgrade.

Node Migration

Another option, temporarily adding nodes for the duration of the release, could mean having more than normal capacity online. Figure 3-5 shows the replacement of all the current app servers with a new set of app servers with the newer software deployed.

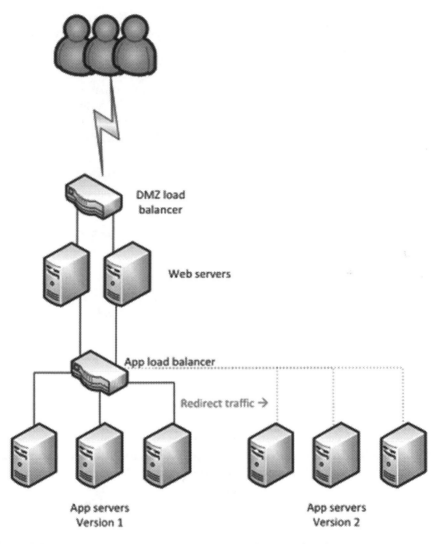

Figure 3-5. Replacing existing application servers with updated application servers

Dark Releases

Software execution that the user is unaware of is a *dark release*. Forthcoming application functionality testing that is hidden from the user interface is an effective way to vet software in production without customer knowledge. Think about a web mail application that includes a chat window. Through settings, you should be able to select whether to see the chat window. The process of loading your people connections with their online status fits the dark release model, in which the application builder can validate that the chat application functions properly and then expose the chat window through the user interface. The same code that allows you to select whether to make the chat window visible was likely used to control the dark release testing, with the toggle also being added to the user interface.

The next time you notice that you are waiting for a web page to load, yet the screen is not changing, ask yourself, "Could dark release code be executing?" And just in case, update your virus and malware software! There are few things more disconcerting than your computer doing a whole bunch of work when you think it should be idle.

Database Release

Not all database code can or should be integrated into the application release automation. Changes being made to a legacy database of record may not be compatible or executable through DevOps automation. Still, a primary edict of DevOps is to automate as much as possible, including configuration files, connection files, and, of course, associated validation test scripts. As code is decoupled from the database, database changes become less risky and they better fit DevOps automation.

Landscape Evolution

A fair estimate is that the majority of currently practicing corporate DBAs cut their teeth on relational databases. From a data access perspective, SQL calls over JDBC, ODBC, a lower-level call interface, or a vendor-provided client-server communication protocol are expected. Sure, there are plenty of DBAs who work in "born on the cloud" organizations that may not be able to spell *relational* because their experience has primarily been with NoSQL databases. These DBAs may have a DevOps head start over the former, but the lead is not insurmountable. Bottom line: data is still data. The way data is stored and accessed may be different, but DBAs remain responsible for data security, availability, consistency, access, performance, recoverability, and more. More on NoSQL databases is coming. Here, microservices and containerization need delving into to help understand landscape evolution.

Microservices

Microservices, just the next evolution of web services, further disassembles code to make smaller, function-oriented code modules. One benefit of web services that corporate DBAs see is the transformation in which monolithic applications are being deconstructed (pulling out specific functions) to increase code manageability, isolate release dependencies, and improve business agility by delivering products faster with less risk. Expect it to take years for a huge application to become fully dismantled, and that is only if the organization acts purposely and aggressively.

Web services are now being looked at from an integration and deployment perspective, in which even these smaller code units are too large to release on the fly, so breaking down web services into microservices enables faster, less risky software updates. For DBAs, how does that impact database access? For instance, the monolithic application may have started out as a client-server implementation that was transformed into a three-tier architecture with connection pools between the application tier and database maintaining live, reusable connections that grew and shrank based on load demand. Then web services entered the picture, with requests hitting the database very frequently, hopefully reusing existing connections.

Containerization

Physical servers started out running a single OS. As resource use efficiency needed to increase to reduce server costs, virtualization caught hold, allowing multiple guest host servers to exist simultaneously. *Containerization* provides the next level of separation, in which a full OS is not required, and resource provisioning is lightweight. Microservices can run inside containers, but not vice versa. One problem with single OS environments is the risk of processes encroaching on one another, causing instability and failures. Virtualizing guests provides separation between processes, minimizing encroachment. Containers take granularity to another level—a single function running in its very own OS space. Figure 3-6 shows the evolution from a single OS with multiple Java virtual machines (JVMs) (A), to one JVM per OS (B), and to many small containers with the OS and JVM (C).

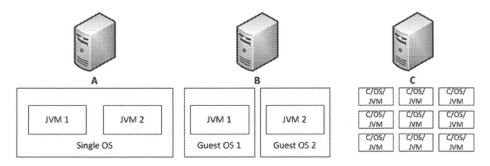

Figure 3-6. Evolution toward containers

Manual to Automatic

Although speed improves pipeline efficiency, initial process changes may be easier to control and evaluate when performed manually. Manually introducing database changes into the agile pipeline provides the time needed to verify the proper sequencing and expected execution, and that follow-on execution steps continue as expected. As confidence builds in the automation and process, and as you learn what the execution looks like (which outputs, errors, and success messages may occur), tuning the process for better error checking, improved execution speed, and sequencing provides opportunities for better craftsmanship for the long haul. Experts are those who have built, tested, failed, rebuilt, resequenced, learned, adjusted, and adapted to the point where they build new products with fewer defects—faster, optimally, and confidently. This leads to higher rates of success because experts know how to avoid pitfalls. Failures seem to reconfigure the brain toward success.

Template Integration

Changes impacting the platform must roll into the build template to maintain consistency. If your organization allows team members to spin-up virtual hosts at will, the base template or database-specific template or add-on needs to quickly evolve to include database changes. Reduced cycle time means that as you are implementing database changes, the pipeline may already be constructed for active backlog work. If the database change has not been incorporated into the build templates, release testing may be occurring with out-of-date database specifications.

Template versioning and source control allows the database infrastructure as code to be synchronized appropriately, which is the evidence for DBAs using source code control. Maintaining database change code in the code repository allows the continuous integration server automation to be configured for database version selection. If the continuous integration server knows that all software releases above version 4.8 require database version 3.9, the code and database can be matched for launch. And if automated template builds know to pull database version 4.1 for software releases 5.2 and greater, it means that hosts spin-ups contain the code and database versions needed for that sprint cycle.

Performance Testing

Performance degradation becomes nearly preventable with excessive testing across consistent platforms. Although many database changes are binary in result (success or failure) and require little time for correction, performance problems enlist us for repetitive, controlled, and prescriptive testing. DevOps' supposition that problems are to be prevented from impacting production—actually ever being pushed into production or the next environment—means that DBAs get the opportunity to correct performance without the added pressure of production impact. The troubleshooting time is not without some pressure because the faster release cycles likely mean that the application change dependent on the problematic database change is quickly approaching release time. Although schedules might adjust to allow time for resolution, not being the bottleneck in product delivery is a matter of pride.

Performance testing becomes "interesting" when the end-state platform is a persistent environment built pre-Agile and pre-DevOps, with all its "quirks" and nonstandard implementations. Of course, adjustments can be made to bring the environment closer in compliance over time by allowing the drift management process to help keep the platform aligned, with fewer and fewer exceptions as time passes. The luxury of building and tearing down virtual hosts as you constantly toil toward implementation perfection is the crash into a brick wall called "the legacy production environment." With that challenge, performance in the pipeline does not, and probably cannot, mirror expectations for production. Working backward from the production implementation to build the nonproduction hosts allows for closer performance results while unfortunately inheriting many noncompliant settings. Production capacity also might not be achievable for the nonprod guests, again presenting risk to be corralled. In other words, the advantages and opportunities presented by DevOps require DBAs to understand that the goal may take years to reach, after persistent and iterative modifications.

Agnostic to the environment, performance problems have to be resolved. Additionally, last month's acceptable performance may not cut it next month. DBAs doing DevOps should now be plugged in to the process earlier, allowing more time to ready the database for the software product changes being driven by the product owner's prioritization of the backlog. Before DevOps, DBAs might have not been aware of changes until nearly release time or worse: postimplementation.

New product search criteria or onboarding a new client representing a 20% increase in business transaction volume are very different performance attributes. The coinciding DBA response must neutralize the potential impact. The response also depends on the database implementation; a new index may be needed for a relational database to meet the new product search criteria performance expectations, whereas a NoSQL database may not require any adjustment because the new search is just another traversing of a data file. Transaction volume increases compute and storage consumption, which may require DBA preparation work; or for a more dynamic environment, automated adjustments may occur as the load increases. Be sure to understand whether or how the environment reacts to load changes, and leverage virtual capabilities for load response and performance management as much as possible. Virtual environment flexibility and adaptability to workload increases and decreases, and performance management using predefined thresholds drive the ROI and total cost of ownership (TCO) numbers that CIOs, and especially CFOs, like to see.

Ascribing to the database vendor's performance investigation recommendations, boosted by years of personal experience, offers substantial performance mitigating and remediation prospects. However, do not forget that the organization has invested in support, not because the company does not think you are capable of maintaining the database; rather, in line with what should be your objective, it provides another path to engage experts to help reduce impact duration. Sure, you want to be the hero by resolving the problem yourself, but if it takes you 12 hours, and engaging the vendor reduces the problem duration to 3 hours, hero becomes a zero. Leverage the support investment to minimize impact; be an availability hero instead of a problem-solving hero.

Test Data

Test data needs to fulfill two purposes: 1) validate the application or database change; and 2) attempt to cause the change to fail. The first data set should be "clean," with each data element fitting properly to the scope of the change. Variety serves only to ensure that each possible data type will process properly in the change context. The second data set is likely to be considered garbage. Every noncompliant data type should be run against the modification that is trying to cause failure. Proper vetting of the data before use should result in an exception or error that could be a true failure; more prosperous would be notification that the data is bad and cannot be used, thus protecting data integrity.

Specific to database data testing, insertions and updates should challenge the column data type. For instance, insert a good value in a column and then try to update the column with a bad value that tests for proper constraint checks or referential integrity where applicable. For code, feeding bad data into a variable, API, or web service call should result in proper error handling, not process failure or data corruption.

Demonstrating sufficient data testing means providing an audit trail that can be communicated and retained as an artifact. If a production problem is caused by malformed data, being able to check test results for missed failures that need to be corrected prior to the next test, or to prove that due diligence was completed yet additional tests are needed, serves team transparency and cooperation rather than finger pointing.

Automated testing creates an efficient data testing capability—being able to process large data sets repetitively, quickly assessing the integrity of the change against data variance.

Summary

DBAs who integrate database changes into existing pipelines should not disrupt the flow or cause cycle times to increase dramatically. Iterative actions that grow the database change automation capability provide time to assess execution and audit the results.

DevOps team members provide the foundational pipeline process and tools that DBAs must learn and ascribe to in order to become an effective DevOps team member. Giving DBAs advice and time to introduce database change automation and infrastructure as code database templates advances the DevOps methodology, which is a win for the organization and its customers.

There are many ways to introduce changes, and this chapter has only scratched the surface. Keep in mind that smaller and more frequent changes minimize risk and allow new features to be implemented faster. Incremental descaling of code segments toward microservices living in containers meets the small change requirement, with a minimal bleed over possibility that may impact other code containers.

Availability and stability are byproducts of the DevOps ideas of excessing testing and small but frequent changes.

Integrating Database Technologies and DevOps Tools

Database technology integration simply involves injecting database automation and database infrastructure as code into the continuous delivery pipeline. The challenge is "where," "when," and "how." Database tool selection criteria must balance database change capability and integration ease with tools already used in pipeline management.

© Michael S. Cuppett 2016

M. S. Cuppett, *DevOps, DBAs, and DBaaS*, DOI 10.1007/978-1-4842-2208-9_4

Rotate Toward Development

Recalling Figure 1-1, you can see that now the App DBA, whether a function or role, must not only shift left to become involved earlier in the process but must also "rotate" toward development to become just another "developer" adding or updating the product code base. Figure 4-1 is Figure 1-1 edited to include the rotate.

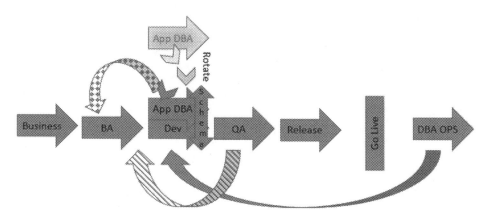

Figure 4-1. Rotating toward development

App DBA work can no longer be a divergent step outside of the SDLC. DBAs initially have much ground to cover before catching up to the automation level attained by development teams using Agile methodologies and early DevOps work, sometimes for years before the DBAs were added (or are to be added) to the DevOps mix. Automating database changes and database installs and configurations takes time and a tremendous testing effort to blend these new DevOps capabilities into the continuous integration (CI) pipeline. The primary measures of progress are the percentage of database work being done using automation and the defect rate. As the percentage of database automation work increases, the defect rate should decrease. Figure 4-2 shows the CI measures.

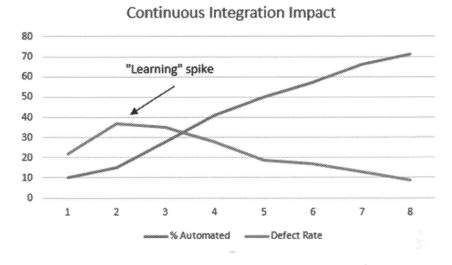

Figure 4-2. CI measures

These two measures should show an inverse correlation. Defect rates may spike early in the automation process as DBAs learn to perfect the code and optimize testing to cover more code and catch additional errors. DevOps team members can expedite DBA progress by communicating lessons learned and best practices for code checking and automation building.

Two key functions, infrastructure as code and source code control, are probably new ideas or processes for many DBAs. Prior to DevOps, a project would be approved and funded, development would start coding, and Operations would get to work "spec-ing" hardware, software, tools, and licensing for the platform. A problem is immediately apparent: Are the developers developing on the target platform? Many times the answer is no, which indicates a high probability of future rework being done to align the software product to the platform, as Figure 4-3 demonstrates.

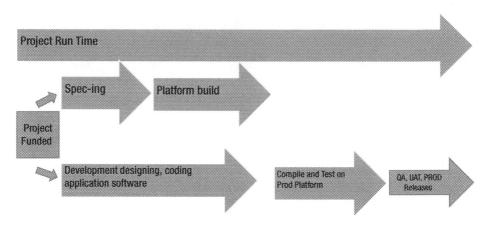

Figure 4-3. Pre-DevOps project example

DevOps turns that model around and has multiple virtual platforms ready for consumption, allowing developers to immediately code with the parameters of the execution platform.

Continuing down the pre-Agile project model path, eventually the pieces needed for the platform are onsite and ready for installation and configuration. Toward the end of this cycle, the DBAs are granted access to the servers for the database software installation. The DBAs have to trust that the build to this point is correct and meets the design specifications for a database host. DBAs start installing the database software, registering the licenses, and preparing a database with proper access control. Tools for managing and monitoring may also be installed during this phase. If multiple servers are built with production, testing, QA, and so on, there is much hope that the builds were completed in the exactly the same way. Variance morphs into disruption too often, causing extended outages and burdensome troubleshooting.

Depending on the amount of code being developed, the development team may have to wait for the platform to be ready for code deployment and testing. In this situation, the business capability is ready for prime time, only to be delayed by cumbersome acquisition and build processes. As mentioned earlier, code issues pertaining to platform incompatibility may come to light, causing rework and further delay (refer to Figure 4-3). The old process has failed and continues to fail the business.

The business was negatively impacted from lost revenue, reduced costs, or improved customer experience; and IT's reputation was tarnished for not understanding the business needs and for slow delivery. DevOps and Agile are rearranging the model.

Resources at the Ready

Whether internally or as a DBaaS, DevOps prepares and provides platforms before projects are started. Once a project (or, more precisely, product work) is ready to begin, development provisions development environments that match the planned production platform (see Figure 4-4).

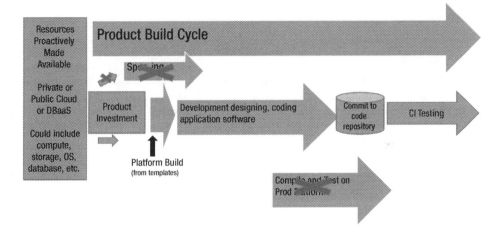

Figure 4-4. Improved and leaner process using virtualization (code repository and CI server added to expand flow)

Virtualization has influenced and empowered this capability. As code development proceeds, additional hosts can be provisioned for testing, again matching the production environment and development environment, which nearly eliminates platform variances that may introduce problems. DBAs play a critical role in platform readiness.

Platform Readiness

Preparing platforms for development and production means that DBAs are doing "infrastructure as code." Moving from physical servers with software installs to leveraging available compute and storage capacity to produce virtual hosts on demand flips the previous model upside down (or, better said, upside right). Key template build steps include verifying prerequisites, building, and auditing for exceptions.

Prerequisites

Determining that all required dependencies are in place before the build execution leads to cleaner builds. Database installs likely require additional and/or different OS components and network configurations than web or application servers do. Process maturity also determines which progressions need to occur before the database build. For instance, SAs may have only base Linux and Windows templates ready for consumption. Alternatively, SAs may have templates covering a broader set of technologies—for example, Windows base, Linux base, Linux Oracle, Windows SQL Server, Windows IIS, and Linux Websphere. This list tells us that the organization's primary or preferred platforms are based on Windows and Linux for the OSs, Oracle and SQL Server for databases, and IIS and Websphere for web/app servers. The expectation is that the delta between the OS base template and the OS database template is that the required packages, compilers, and configuration settings are installed to support the database environment. Figure 4-5 shows a sample template selection interface.

Select one of the following:

- ○ Windows base
- ○ Linux base
- ○ Linux Oracle
- ○ Windows SQL Server
- ○ Windows IIS
- ○ Linux Websphere

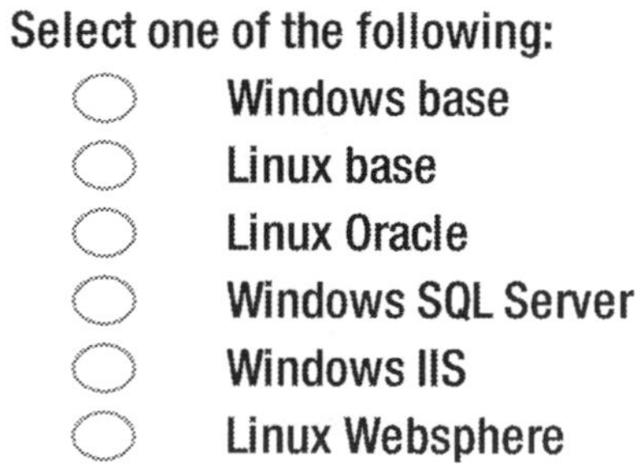

Figure 4-5. Sample template selection interface

Licensing, or license availability, should be a precheck. Whether creating a text file containing a license key or using a software package for reserving and issuing licenses, the "how" matters less than planning for and having a license available for the build process.

Whether for internal consumption, customer product inclusion, or as a Platform as a Service (PaaS) solution, the templates should look very similar. If the templates are tried and true, DBAs may decide to trust the templates and move directly to the build process. For less-mature templates, DBAs should script checks to ensure that the supporting template builds meet database requirements. The database vendor's install process likely includes preinstall and/or prebuild checks that can be leveraged. There is no reason to duplicate effort. After proving that the platform has been built correctly from the template, DBAs can expand the database template.

Build

Having already selected the template intended for the target database eco-system and spinning up a virtual host, the DBA begins to build the install and database build procedures needed for a template. The first install and build can be done manually by recording the information feed into the process to be included in the script. For an Oracle install, a response file can be created to be read by the install process, which may be a technique incorporated into the template. DBAs may first build a secondary template that includes the data-base software install and initial database build. After testing and refining the template, the secondary template should be absorbed into the initial template, reducing the build steps.

The build part of the template needs to be flexible to support planned use cases. There may be a need to have small, medium, and large offerings; or sup-port for single node and clustered nodes needs to be included. Remember that the DBA may not be the person executing the build, so assumptions need to be eliminated. Presenting options to the consumer may be in the form of a GUI interface or having the requestor create a text file containing needed information saved to a specific location.

Build information includes all the information inputted during the manual pro-cess, plus information specific to this particular build. Here are some expected inputs: database name; file location; memory size based on small, medium, or large; license key; logging/archiving; clustering; network port; backup method and retention; and more. As a DBaaS offering, the number of customer inputs should be limited to reduce complexity and template maintenance effort. With internal offerings for which the consumer is likely to be an IT person, the inputs can be increased to be very granular—with the caution that these environments need to be supported, making every difference a potential prob-lem area to be considered during troubleshooting. Leaning toward simplicity is a smart move. Besides, in the virtual world, changing a database from small to larger (or doing the inverse) equates to a few clicks to change the resources made available to the guest host.

Log File

Just as important as it is for the DBA to make sure the prerequisites are in place to support the database software install and initial database build is to make sure that the build completes correctly. The build script should create an extensive log that records *everything*, including customer inputs. Where possible, the logs should be built for easy parsing based on key words such as SUCCESS, FAILED, and so on. Of course, the final steps in the script are automated log checks to report exceptions needing attention. DevOps drives automating as much as possible to reduce variances from human error.

Additionally, the audit log may be needed when responding to internal and/or external governing bodies to check compliance for SOX, PCI-DSS, HIPAA, and so on. Be sure to archive the audit logs aligned with organizational or governing body data retention requirements.

The effort expended in building and testing everything needed to implement the templates is designing infrastructure as code. Infrastructure is no longer a physical server with rigid controls; instead, servers are virtual hosts that can be built and destroyed repeatedly. Developers, DevOps engineers, and DBAs can easily experiment (take risks) with new code approaches and alternate configurations to test performance, stability, and more by building "infrastructure" using code—executing the appropriate template. Having a pool of resources at the ready eliminates the wait time most likely to stall a project, preventing new functionality from getting to the customer, and delaying the business' ROI.

Source Code Control

All scripts included in the database templates must be managed using the same source code control software as the software product code (see Figure 4-6).

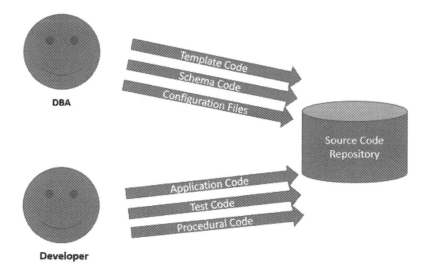

Figure 4-6. Source code repository for application and database code

DBAs need to check code in and out just like the developers do, and database changes need to be managed in the same manner. The build templates may not be part of the CI process because these builds pertain to hosts, not the software product. People needing a new database host execute the needed template and they are in business. Database changes, such as stored procedures, index creates or drops, and schema object changes should be part of the CI process.

The primary difference in the CI process for database changes is when the database changes are introduced. CI is simply an automated process that checks to make sure that new, modified, or removed (which seems counterintuitive, but can have impact) code can play nice with all the other code comprising the product. Developers should always be working on the more important backlog priorities, being able to commit code immediately upon completion. For DBAs, adding an index to correct a known performance issue that can be included in any version of the software product can be tested immediately during the next CI run once the index code is committed. In contrast, changing a table or modifying a collection requires delicate timing for inclusion in the product, in conjunction with the supporting code change. Recall from the last chapter that Figure 3-3 provided an example of database change timing mixed with application updates.

Database changes can be introduced in a dormant state, ready for activation once the supporting code is in place. Toggling the code base allows multiple code versions to be in place, ready to go live with the database changes. Let's say you have promised your customers new functionality that involves new columns or attributes that need to be stored in the database to be live on October 23. Previously, an outage was probably planned for the evening of October 22 to implement needed changes so that the new features could come online at 12:00 a.m. on October 23. However, for this application, you are required to have the system available 24x7x365, no exceptions. How do you implement changes? The reality is that making database changes without at least a short outage is nearly impossible without significant investment, but durations can be shortened using automation.

Availability also needs to be defined. Does having a read-only database available for queries fit the requirement? If writes are required, could all changes be captured on the secondary database for inclusion in the primary database once it is available?

Metadata changes——whether a switch or key field text——are frequently used for application settings. Metadata changes can also manage other configuration settings. For example, one entry could simply be the code version to be executed. With that, somewhere in the code a read of the metadata to determine how to execute based on the defined code version. As shown in the example, at 12:00 a.m. on October 23 an update (automated hopefully) to the metadata to change the code version activated the expected customer features. That takes care of the code, but what steps need to be taken to activate the database changes?

Database changes may be as simple as changing a column or attribute from null to not null, making the new data element mandatory. Trickier changes such as a table reorganization—maybe the lead column is new—require much more work to implement. Creating a new table, pulling in the data from the old table version with the lead column data added (see Figure 4-7) and then renaming the old table to .old and renaming the new table to be the production table name can all be done with automation.

Table (old version)	Table (new version)
Column 1 Emp_ID (PK)	ID (generated PK)
Column 2 Emp_First_Name	Emp_ID
Column 3 Emp_Last_Name	Emp_First_Name
Column 4	Emp_Last_Name

Figure 4-7. Table change example

The larger challenge is table size, which is one reason why DBAs should make sure that a good archive process is in place to keep the table row count manageable.

New tables that may have been implemented months ago but left dormant until needed are also manageable in conjunction with code activation. Now as the new code version is being implemented, the dormant table starts being used. The orchestration must be precise, ensuring that the code and table activations are synced. If the new table is just new and needed for a new functional requirement, the work is complete. However, if the new table exists to replace a table or tables, the data transfer is included in the orchestration automation. Be very careful to identify and resolve all dependencies and code references, or use aliases where feasible.

Tables that had been active could also be excluded from the new code version, going dormant pending archiving and destruction decisions.

Today's always-on customer expectations require new thinking to drive "live" implementations models, even for legacy systems that might need to be dismantled—pulling out functions that can be replaced by API calls or services. As the legacy code base shrinks, implementations begin to shrink as fewer and fewer changes are needed for the code release.

Understanding Change Failures

Although this section discusses production specifically, the lessons apply to all environments in the release process. In a perfect DevOps world, environments always remain true to the release version, anticipating the next version deployment. In the real world of production, things can get skewed as teams react to business-impacting events and make changes outside of the deployment cycle. From the DevOps perspective, "surprise" production problems equal failure. Depending on the deployment method, these changes are at risk of repeating failures. If deployments include building the hosts from infrastructure as code templates followed by an application release, the modifications made to production to keep the business running get excluded, meaning that the new deployment immediately risks operations.

Preventing this scenario comes in at least three flavors. First, production changes outside of the release process are never made, period. This requires a mature deployment process that allows high-priority changes to be tested and deployed very quickly. This process may be considered an exception path in the deployment mechanism, having a modified and probably shortened process flow that expedites changes necessary to correct the production problem or performance issue. Because the code associated with the corrective action was released through the deployment pipeline, the code has been captured for inclusion in the next release.

Second, changes made to production must be communicated back to development for inclusion in the code base, with full testing to finish vetting the change. This process requires a formal change request that tracks the problem, the cause, the corrective action, and the name of the person who made the change. The change request can then be managed from the back log, ensuring inclusion in the code trunk.

Third is the best-suited scenario for this situation and for general releases: the build process needs to compare the source (new version), the target (environment to be deployed to), and the baseline code version (last release). For example, if deploying code version 5, it is necessary to ensure that the deployed-to environment does not lose code that may have been put into place to correct a problem. The best case is that the code base equals version 4 perfectly. When a difference is discovered, questions need to be raised to determine why the difference exists and how the difference needs to be handled.

You should be able to rectify every difference for the version 4 and 5 code bases, hopefully so that each change is expected and has been tracked through the change process. This is expected. We also expect that comparing version 5 to the environment to be deployed to will reveal differences. What is not expected is comparing version 4 to the environment to be deployed to and finding differences. The differences can vary. For instance, version 4 may not have a foreign key that is in the deployed environment. Finding out why should be easy enough if the change request process is being used to track all changes. If the foreign key was added to solve a problem, it needs to remain in place. The next question should be, "Does version 5 include the foreign key?" Proper change management should have driven this change into version 5. If not, the foreign key code needs to be merged into version 5 before deployment. Consider this requirement when vetting tools or be sure to script or manually perform these checks.

Finally, Tools and Databases

Tools enable DevOps (and Agile) to increase productivity, decrease errors, lean out non-value-added steps, maintain an audit trail, and (most importantly from my performance-obsessed perspective) do everything really fast! Let's delve into a variety of popular nonrelational databases, followed by a few DevOps tools. Be sure to visit each product's web site for full details.

Nonrelational Databases

NoSQL gets interpreted as "No SQL" and "Not Only SQL," depending on an author's experience or perspective. The latter appears to be more accurate.

Relational databases remain the "entrée" on the table for companies that are heavily invested in larger server platforms, database software, and licensing. The shift in these companies are NoSQL databases going from hors d'oeuvres to becoming hearty side dishes, a signal of gaining prominence. One primary circumstance requires looking no further than the DevOps movement. The speed and accuracy encompassing DevOps create the opportunity to consider different database types when searching for optimal performance and agility. Nonrelational data storage is less stringent than relational storage, making schemas more malleable in the former.

Key information covering four relatively popular NoSQL databases follows.

MongoDB (www.mongodb.com)

MongoDB is an aggregate-oriented, key-value database that actually leverages the maturity of relational database technology combined with NoSQL capabilities to have the best of both worlds, referred to as the Nexus Architecture.

Data is stored as collections (tables) that contain documents (rows) with each data element in a field (columns). Fields can be added to documents without having to first declare the structure, a process known as *self-describing*. It is not required to include the same fields, so it makes the "schema" flexible. MongoDB supports document create, read, update, delete (CRUD) operations and stores the data as binary JavaScript Object Notation (JSON), a data interchange format.

MongoDB comes in several distributions, each offering a different set of tools and capabilities: security, management and operations, encryption, auditing, and auto-sharding to scale linearly.

▓ **Note** *Sharding* entails dividing a database into smaller partitions (*shards*) for faster and easier management. It is a method to horizontally scale a database across multiple host servers.

Couchbase (www.couchbase.com)

Couchbase is an aggregate-oriented NoSQL, distributed architecture, JSON document database that improves developer transitions from relational databases through the use of SQL, the syntax being very closely aligned. Features include flexible data modeling, indexing, SQL migration to leverage existing relational database queries, security, and monitoring deployment and administration. Couchbase has buckets at its top-level namespace.

Cassandra (cassandra.apache.org)

An aggregate-oriented, NoSQL wide-column, distributed data store featuring fault tolerance (no single point-of-failure for 100% availability), scalability, and high performance using distributed identical nodes. Tools, the Cassandra Query Language (CQL), data modeling, security, compression, and change data capture round out this database. Cassandra's top-level namespace is a key-space used to hold tables or column families.

Neo4J (www.neo4j.com)

Unlike the previous three examples, Neo4j stands out as a product specifically designed as a graph database in which data relationships are valued over the data itself. Nodes (e.g., people, places, or things) and the relationships between nodes can be used to model patterns or scenarios. For instance, a data pattern can be identified to help detect fraud. If two people (nodes) in different locations use the same Social Security number to open new credit accounts, something is amiss. Social networks can make friend or group recommendations by looking at similarities in what you "like," where you live, the college you attended, people you are already connect with, and your hobby—matched to other people with nearly the same data points.

Neo4j uses the atomic, consistent, isolated, durable (ACID) consistency model common for relational databases, and it supports CRUD. Features include native graph storing and processing, data import, flexible schema, a full suite of drivers, tools, and the Cypher query language.

Note These databases and other competing products offer many overlapping capabilities that were purposely not included. Please take time to evaluate many products. These products tend to use different names for the same objects; for example, *containers*, *buckets*, and *keyspace* describe top-level namespaces.

Tools

Tools are booster rockets strapped to DevOps. DevOps is changing culture and processing to create better software products and platforms. To help do that really, really fast, tools make it possible to automate and orchestrate pipeline work and flow.

Key information covering three relatively popular tools follows.

Jenkins (https://jenkins.io/)

Jenkins is an automation server for CI though continuous delivery. Extendible by using plug-ins, the architecture supports integration to most tools, work can be distributed across nodes, and there is an easy setup and configuration using a web interface.

Once Jenkins is running, a pipeline (workflow) can be created to build, test, and deliver products. Jenkins CI kicks in after code has been committed to the repository. Jenkins can be used to check out software; grab dependent code; build/compile/launch code segments (it works with Docker); run testing from individual modules to end-to-end testing; and, if warranted, deploy the new code version into the different environments. A full reportable audit is produced as the code progresses through the pipeline.

Jenkins supports pipeline as code, which enables the workflow definition to be managed by the code repository, allowing changes to be tracked and implemented.

Chef (www.chef.io/)

Chef is also an automation server. Full DevOps automation can be achieved to process application code from source control, through testing, and to deployment with a full audit trail from which to report. Chef promises transformation to a software-driven organization using extensive collaboration and automation.

InSpec provides a framework for security and compliance inclusion, ensuring that the software meets the requirements. Habitat delivers the ability for apps to run anywhere by "traveling" with the software to make it capable of running on bare metal, PaaS, VMs, and containers.

TeamCity (`www.jetbrains.com/teamcity/`)

TeamCity, which uses the moniker "Your 24/7 Build Engineer," is a CI platform. TeamCity is extendible via plug-ins (or you can create your own plug-ins using the provided API), so it is a flexible environment. Supporting many programming languages fits most integration and deployment needs.

Covering CI, delivery, and deployment, TeamCity provides a scalable architecture to progress the work efficiently.

▓ **Note**   As mentioned for the databases, these and competing products offer many overlapping features, which are not discussed here. Investigate many products in light of your requirements. Terminology varies, so be sure you understand what the terms represent.

When selecting DevOps tools and nonrelational databases, be sure that each supports the planned programming language. The production combination selection is as important as the individual product selections.

Databases and Tools—So Happy Together

Because there is a plethora of nonrelational databases, an organization's existing relational databases, and plenty of automation and orchestration platform offerings, matching products well can decrease the learning curve and speed up the integration process, allowing for quicker wins and financial returns. Many (probably most) DBAs and DevOps team members have worked with a variety of tools throughout their careers, which makes adapting to DevOps tools relatively easy. Even command-line commandos can quickly increase tool use proficiency while providing the extra capability of reviewing, understanding, and editing scripts directly.

Doing DevOps

One of the coolest things about DevOps is that with automation and orchestration you can literally build, test, and destroy any combination of database, fully testing the application code against each database in the search for the most optimal product teaming. You may need to install APIs for the CI servers, but that is still a small effort for a large reward.

Another test is to extract data from a relational database into a NoSQL database to determine whether read times can be increased for certain queries, especially when the reads result in few writes. For example, if a report needs to read "tons" of data from a relational database, it might be worth a look at redesigning the report to extract data from a new document NoSQL database. The NoSQL database could be populated over time by forwarding transactions from the relational database, spreading the load across hours, for the report to access—potentially on a different server than the relational database.

I say it again: DevOps allows you to do really cool testing on the quest for the best solution. A pilot becomes an exponentially more comprehensive evaluation because automation and orchestration can be leveraged to perform build, conduct testing, and move on to the next configuration.

Summary

DevOps has a slew of database and tools options that are all purposed to build, automate, and orchestrate the code pipeline. DBAs need to evaluate options for integrating database builds and changes into the code repository and pipeline work flow. The challenge is to not disrupt code progression, introduce database changes and testing, and improve the cycle time. As database changes become automated and orchestrated, cycle time should decrease, making it possible to deliver products faster.

Stateful Data, Stateless Database Schema, and Code

Stateful and stateless programming can be defined as software code that maintains a state or data element, or sees each interaction without previous context. *Stateful programming* is the dominate sibling because any time a variable is set (i=1), a data element is captured (for example, capturing customer order information on an e-commerce site), a variable in a loop is incremented, or an array is used, a state is present. In and of itself, stateful is not a problem because state is needed for many transactional interactions. DevOps does not mandate that all code must become stateless, but there are times when stateless brings opportunity.

© Michael S. Cuppett 2016

M. S. Cuppett, *DevOps, DBAs, and DBaaS*, DOI 10.1007/978-1-4842-2208-9_5

Stateless programming is growing as containerization, microservices, and DevOps are growing because code segments need to execute in parallel without dependency on another code segment. Because code can execute without dependency, it becomes easier to update the code without impacting other pieces of the system. If each container is autonomous, then creation, change, or the destruction of it or surrounding containers has zero effect on the rest.

To maintain transaction progress information, a stateful object (such as a cookie for a web interaction) may be used to keep track of the interaction. An API or microservices call made within a transaction flow, in which the requested data is not required for recall later in the program, should be stateless because there is no reason to maintain a state. Doing a search from a browser is stateless because the search engine finds matching information and sends it to the requester. The search engine then waits for the next instruction without referencing the previous query. NoSQL database implementations are growing as organizations need agility and speed in response to customer demands. Delivering and capturing data without the stringent relational database normalization and predefined scheme object definitions, NoSQL databases are answering the call with simpler and faster implementations, lower costs, and "schemas" that are adaptable in real time.

All this flexibility helps DevOps improve implementations by removing dependencies (stateless objects do not care about others) and eliminating or minimizing deployment outages.

Network "States"

Discussions about stateful and stateless application code are relatively new. Fortunately, stateful and stateless network protocols have existed for decades, allowing us to better understand this newer topic by building on information that is already understood. Transmission Control Protocol (TCP) and User Datagram Protocol (UDP) have many differences, but for our context the focus is on the concepts of *connection-oriented* and connectionless-oriented.

TCP establishes a session between two computers that is maintained until the conversation completes. For instance, when you execute "ftp *<server name>*, the connection between your client computer and the host identified in *<server name>* is established using TCP. File Transfer Protocol (FTP) establishes a session over the connection for the duration of the file transfer until the session is closed. TCP is connection-oriented, or stateful, because the protocol keeps the information needed to maintain and reestablish the connection.

UDP was also used in the FTP example, but indirectly. When the FTP command executes, a call was made to a Domain Name Server (DNS) to translate the *<server name>* into an IP address. The request was sent in the hope that an answer would be provided. UDP is stateless because it does not require a connection; once it executes, it does not wait for a response.

The FTP example shows stateful and stateless in the context of network connectivity, which constructs a foundation on which you can build.

Live Implementations

Keeping an application available while making database changes can be tricky, but not undoable. Some environments are more complicated, perhaps complex enough to warrant not doing live implementations. A monolithic legacy application or vendor enterprise resource planning (ERP) system may not be worth the effort to make live implementations palatable. Complexity impedes DevOps; therefore, it is imperative that simplification become a mandate as the organization pushes forward with DevOps.

Smaller, Agile-developed, and uncomplicated applications provide reasonable opportunities for live implementations, stemming from the initial database design consideration for continuous availability. Application segmentation—API calls, web services, containerization, and microservices—sanctions application updates to be done in real time; and operating an application while doing software updates is becoming the standard, which stirs companies to accelerate simplification and application segmentation. Reaching the same point for making database changes "live" requires rethinking database availability, the database model, and (most importantly) the database. Whether graph or document, a database may be a better fit than a relational database, so determining the best database for the job is important for availability.

Redefining Availability

Many IT professionals still view application and database availability as a single event. The application and database are so tightly coupled that customers cannot use the environment without each running. Agile development and DevOps are working to change the perception that it has to be that way by providing methods to reduce application and database dependencies. The path forward is rethinking how to store data distributively and how to segment applications into more manageable parts.

From a business perspective, an application is available when the application can be used—data can be viewed, edited, and submitted—to perform business functions. Monolithic applications are assigned uptime and performance requirements that are determined by the more critical functions. As applications are deconstructed, the individual parts have different uptime and performance requirements.

Understanding how the data is used, which data is involved, and integration dependencies allows application work to be broken down into functional purposes, making it possible to draw a line in the sand for availability. Again, this segregation may not be feasible for monolithic applications with single-schema databases and vendor ERP systems.

As organizations decouple applications from databases, options become available to better manage data and availability. Migrating data from a relational database into a NoSQL database to decrease customer query times is a good move. Product queries are made faster by searching denormalized data in a NoSQL database; when the interaction moves to purchase, the relational database can be used to record the transaction.

Content management applications or in-memory databases share a goal: provide information quickly. However, each product is backed by a master data source or single point of truth database, which requires the applications to check for changes before delivering the result. If a change has occurred, the updated information has to be copied to refresh the local data before being delivered to the requester. The performance improvement for 99.9% of inquires accounts for the fact that the information is relatively static.

Here's another example: the first time you visit a web site, it is likely to be slower than an immediate reload because the initial request has to download images, Java scripts, and so on. On the reload, the browser is aware of the images stored locally, it makes a quick call to see whether the image has changed; if not, it loads the image from the local cache instead of pulling the image across the network.

Instead of depending on a single database, architectures can adapt to business demand by considering the idea that data can be positioned strategically to improve application performance. The caveat is to make sure you have planned how to maintain data integrity. A master database management repository can be used to "correct" data in other databases.

Everything mentioned here requires extensive planning, automation building, and testing because it is not easy. IT shops have been taking outages for decades to implement database and code changes, so do not expect overnight miracles.

Functional Data Requirements

Let's use a product–ordering web site as an example. The primary data elements are customer, product, order, and payment. Unless this is the only application for your company, there are probably several databases supporting this application. For this example, each data element is stored in a separate database: customer database, product database, order database, and payment database. When a customer visits the web site, the application has to know about the customer or be able to register the customer and product inventory needs to be available for the customer to browse. Of course, the order has to be anticipated and generated, and payment needs to be taken.

Stateful Data

Data integrity remains a mandate, no matter how a database change is implemented. Keeping with our example, it seems straightforward that the relational database presents the least risk to modify, while the product database keeps the application available. Maintaining the data does not mean that the data can be only in its "home" database. If the application architecture includes a data-caching layer, caching the data may be an option. For the duration of a database update, product update loads can be suspended, and the cache can be allowed to become stale. The code would have to support providing data to the customer while the source data cannot be checked for newer information,

Loading data into a NoSQL database may also be an option. The application must already be configured to use the alternate database, which means that the database connection code needs to be in place and "toggle-able." Steps for this change include loading the product data into the NoSQL database and toggling the application to use the NoSQL database for product queries. Code abstraction and dynamic queries make this easier.

Additionally, you may have chosen at some point to maintain a copy to the product database in a DBaaS solution. Updates made to the primary database would be sent to the secondary database. In this case, the application could be pointed to the secondary database while the primary database is being updated, followed by the application being directed back the primary database for the secondary database to be modified.

No matter the reason, when the opportunity to use a NoSQL database arises and you decide to execute, be sure to consider the pros and cons for staying on NoSQL. A product database seems like an excellent fit for a NoSQL implementation.

Note Agreed, the data can also be loaded into another relational database, but because the intent of this book is to discuss managing a variety of data platforms, I went with the NoSQL route.

Code Abstraction

Although DBAs frequently work with code abstraction, they may not look at it as code abstraction. *Code abstraction* reduces the need to understand everything about a function or other capabilities. An application needing a print option does not require the developer to write a print function; instead, the programming language includes a library of common functions that provides the code behind the scenes. The developer needs to code only the print function name and variable: `print (x)`, for example. Most development languages offer a `print()` function.

Software libraries are a great example of code abstraction. For the next example, let's use an Oracle TNS connection setup. The DBA configures and starts the LISTENER on the database server without seeing what the LISTENER code looks like. The LISTENER function does not need to be understood by the DBA for the DBA to be able to activate it. On the client side, a `tnsnames.ora` file is constructed with connection information needed to reach the LISTENER on the database server. Whether Oracle SQLPlus or an application riding on an ODBC or JDBC connection is used, the underlying software initiates the connection to the database without the DBA seeing the code.

DBAs can look at application code and support the database, all while knowing little about the database software. Yes, you can do a trace on an OS process ID to see read and write calls, but not the actual code.

Code abstraction makes it possible to develop APIs and services for customers or partners to interact with an organization without exposing an application that might include intellectual property. All the customer or partner needs to know is what to expect from the interface and how to "speak" to the API or service. We interface with these types of transactions more than we realize.

When you pay for your snack using your cell phone, you can surmise what is happening, but you cannot see behind the scenes. All you know or probably care about is that once the total charge is revealed, your phone talks to the magic box attached to the register for purchase approval.

Even nonautomated interchanges can be used as analogies. For example, as you are moving into your new house or leased apartment, you contact utility, phone, cable, satellite (for us old-schoolers), and security system companies to have the services installed or activated. As far as your API or service interaction—a phone call or web site submission—is concerned, all you care about is having services turned on within a few days at most. How the electricity, gas, water, television signal, and the rest get to your place is likely not your concern.

API and web service usage come with the same expectation: a request is made and the expected outcome happens. DevOps wants to break interactions into even smaller elements so that services can be updated immediately without impacting ongoing transactions.

Dynamic Queries

A simple SQL query is just a request for data (select *<data>*) from a specific data location (from *<tablename>*), usually with a filter to reduce the return data set (where *<filters>*); for example, select product_name from product where product_id = 100. Assuming that this data exists, the product name with matching product ID is returned for the requester to view. This simple query can perhaps be "hard-coded" into the application when there is no concern that the database may change. The need for dynamic queries is driven by the possibility that the database containing the data may change. The data may be stored in a relational database that is then loaded into a NoSQL database to be used by the same application. Two code versions could be included in the application, with a precheck that determines which code to use, based on a metadata setting defining the database or database connection information. What if a third database comes into play? Does a code version need to be built for each possible database, or does having a SQL code version and a document code version provide everything needed? Maybe these questions do not need to be answered because that goes against the need to simplify.

Building dynamic queries is just code that builds code for execution. The application has to interrogate the database to determine how to build the query. Previously, a query to get the product name from the product table having a specific product ID was shown. What happens when the product data is pulled into a different database that has different data properties? Maybe the data is stored in a MongoDB database in which collections equal tables and documents equal rows. MongoDB's "select" looks like a programming language function call: db.products.find(). MongoDB's find() method equals select in SQL. Knowing that there are many differences in terminology, making the application code use the correct query format is a matter of knowing the data source and data element needed.

▓ **Note**   Consider these code examples pseudo code because it is presumed that each reader knows how to formulate queries and or is capable of searching for examples. The $ sign is used to identify a variable; be sure to use the correct syntax for your programming language.

The SQL query we used:

```
select product_name
from product
where product_id = 100;
```

The NoSQL query would be something like:

```
db.products.find(
{ product_id: 100}
{product_name:  1, _id:  0}
)
```

For this example, a metadata setting is used to define the database that is currently active.

`Database = MongoDB` (the metadata cannot be stored in the database)

The user has already provided the needed input by entering the product ID in the web site search window: `$product_id = 100`. At this point, the application knows what information is needed and from which database.

Variable in play:

```
$product_name = null
$product_id = 100   (user inputted)
$object_name = product (location in code execution for product query)
$Database = MongoDB
```

The code builds a query statement variable using this general syntax:

```
$statement = db.$object_name.find(
{ product_id: $product_id}
        {product_name:  1, _id:  0}
```

Changing the metadata to use a SQL database: `Database = SQL`

The code builds a query statement variable using this general syntax:

```
$statement = Select product_name
from $object_name
where product_id = $product_id;
```

The application then executes the statement `execute $statement return $product_name`, expecting the product name to be returned for display to the user.

Many code variations can be created to build dynamic code to execute against different databases or non–database data sources to not limit the possibilities.

Stateless Database Schema

Stateless database schema is a misnomer in that NoSQL databases do not always use the term *schema* (instead, it uses *collections*). However, because most DBAs becoming involved in DevOps are coming from relational database management environments, *schema* is used to reflect and communicate how dynamic "schemas" can be used in DevOps.

As discussed, data must be stateful, protected, and not inadvertently manipulated as it is moved between databases and other formats. Just like copying data between Microsoft Office products, the data has to remain exactly the same—only the presentation layer changes. Taking a snapshot of Excel spreadsheet data for inclusion in a PowerPoint deck demonstrates stateless environments for stateful data.

Examples of stateless database schema include extract, transform, load (ETL) and analytic data grabs. Data is pulled out of one schema and loaded into a new schema—transformed as needed for the new environment. The data values remain the same; they are being used as the base data that can be transformed and aggregated for analysis. Transactional data is a recording of events that has to be transformed to identify patterns and trends needed to understand how products, customers, locations, and other markers compare with peers.

In DevOps, data needs to be in the best database or container befitting the work at hand. Speed and agility need to be the primary drivers for data retrieval and manipulation. Customers—internal or external—expect applications to perform without noticeable delays. Waiting for screens to change and watching the cursor "spin" frustrates users. Preventing data retrieval or manipulation from being part of the delay demands selecting and implementing the best database for the job. Over the years, relational databases were abused, with square data being forced into circular holes. This process has never worked well; instead, it met the cost side of the equation—not wanting to invest where millions already had been. That unfit use of relational databases for unstructured data management is now being unwound, shifting unstructured data into databases designed specifically for nonrelational data models.

The schema limitation and the response are succinctly defined by the MongoDB team:

> *Schema design determines the way an application handles its data. With traditional relational databases, you must define your schema before you can add any data. This inflexibility means you can't change your schema as your data, application requirements or business evolves. In today's world hyper-competitive, global business environment, this can hamper your efforts to innovate and stay on top of the competition. NoSQL databases arose to address this limitation by allowing you to insert data without a predefined schema. Because of this, you can easily make changes to an application without interruption. The result is more reliable code integration, faster development, and database administration time.*[1]

---

[1]https://www.mongodb.com/scale/dynamic-schema-design

Relational database tables are created with the essential data attributes included in the definition. To add or change a column definition requires altering the table to set a new data type. NoSQL documents are not required to have the same data, data type, or data size in every document within a collection, which results in documents not containing all the data that might be in other documents. Let's compare a relation table to a NoSQL document.

Relational Table Column Names

```
HOBBIST_ID
HOB_FIRST_NAME
HOB_LAST_NAME
FAV_HOBBY_ONE
FAV_HOBBY_TWO
FAV_HOBBY_THREE
```

All the previous columns accept character data; the first four columns are required, and the last two columns are optional. In a relational database, a CREATE TABLE statement is executed to define the table as described. A DBA can quickly look at the table definition to know that each record includes an ID, first and last name, and up to three listed hobbies.

To create a NoSQL document, the data is just entered using the field : value construct. You can also create the document and then add it to a collection or you can add a document directly into a collection:

Example document

```
{
"HOBBIST_ID" : "1",
"HOB_FIRST_NAME" : "Super",
"HOB_LAST_NAME" : "Nerd",
"FAV_HOBBY_ONE" : "NoSQL"
}
```

Documents in a collection are not required to contain the same or all fields. A query searching for a value in FAV_HOBBY_TWO or FAV_HOBBY_THREE would not find a value in the previous document. Also, a DBA looking at one document cannot conclude that every document contains the same data because there is no requirement to maintain a placeholder for the additional information.

> *Developers have typically had to add application-side code to enforce data quality controls, such as mandating the presence of specific fields, data types or permissible values. More sophisticated NoSQL databases allow validation rules to be applied within the database, allowing users to enforce governance across data, while maintaining the agility benefits of a dynamic schema.*[2]

---

[2]https://www.mongodb.com/nosql-explained

As quoted, the relational database schema definition benefits of data validation and required data elements are not lost when deploying a NoSQL database solution.

Being able to add a field and value, which dynamically changes the schema, is why NoSQL databases provide the flexibility needed in DevOps environments. Adding a document with a new field (column) into a collection looks like this:

```
db.hobbist.insert( {"HOBBIST_ID" : "10",
"HOB_FIRST_NAME" : "Uber",
"HOB_LAST_NAME" : "Geek"
"FAV_HOBBY_ONE" : "Writing",
"NEW_FIELD" : "NEW_VALUE"
} )
```

Adding a column to a relational database table requires an ALTER TABLE command that would cause a temporary locking of the table until the change is completed, which would be noticed by application users. This type of change is usually done during a planned outage or designated change window.

Stateful Code

Code that remembers values, state, or previous interactions is considered stateful, leaving stateless code to be defined as code that does not remember values, maintain state, or remember processing history. Functions make excellent examples for showing the difference between different coding practices, even stateful versus stateless. Most programming languages define *functions* as code that performs discrete instructions, as opposed to procedures that may include decisions, keep variable information, or complete multiple tasks. Functions execute in isolation and independently, making them easy to include in programs when specific work needs to be completed. Although not every function is stateless, discerning the state is not as difficult as determining state for larger code segments.

Programming languages and even desktop productivity tools provide common functions. In Excel, you can use the AVERAGE() function to get the average value for a set of numbers, as shown in Figure 5-1.

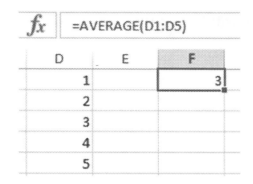

Figure 5-1. Excel AVERAGE() function example

Figure 5-2 shows a different number of inputs, yet the function still returns the average value.

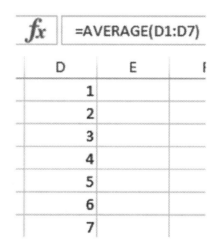

Figure 5-2. Excel AVERAGE() function example with a larger data set

Figure 5-2 makes it apparent that the AVERAGE() function in Excel allows a variable number of inputs without code modification. The AVERAGE() function executes each time with no memory of past executions—it is an example of stateless code.

Returning to the Excel example shown in Figure 5-2, the number of values to be used comes from counting the number of cells in the range D1:D7 that equal 7; the values to be averaged are the content in each cell (1,2,3,4,5,6,7).

Variable assignments reflect stateful code because the variable could be referenced again, producing an output value.

Stateful code makes it difficult to change the environment without interrupting in-progress transactions.

Stateless Code

The independency of stateless code, especially running in a container, relieves the change burden. Let's start with the back end being a NoSQL document database. Because documents do not have fixed structures like tables and do not need to contain the same data element, new documents can be added to a collection without any change to the database.

Starting simply, here is a simple stateless function to print the input value passed to the function:

Note   Pseudo code only.

```
function print_input (parameter)
      print (parameter)
end
```

A stateless function to print a random value follows:

```
function print_random ()
      print(rand())
end
```

Notice that both examples lack variable assignments. Each function performs one task with no context of what happened in a previous execution or concern with the next execution. Also, the function does not contain a session reference.

The first function allows a single input and produces a single output. If the functions code was not contained within a function, instead entangled in a larger program, making a change to print two values would cause the entire program to be implemented as a change.

The second function prints a random value. Again, when embedded in a larger program, making a change involves the larger program. Fortunately, the function is containerized.

Continuing with the containerized code scenario, an audit record is created and written to the database near the end of the application process flow. So far, stateful. However, a random number must be appended to the record to meet a new security requirement.

The record written to the file is compiled from data known the application (stateful) and a random number that is generated from using the rand() function (stateless). Here is the print statement:

```
print (value 1, value 2, value 3, rand())
```

As mentioned, this data is written to a document in a NoSQL database. A requirement change comes from the legal department, requiring a more impressive random value to replace the current random value. Because the function is containerized, and there are many containers running with the function, the change can be made without an outage or customers even noticing.

Change the function by replacing rand() with moreimpressiverand() and deploy the code in a container for testing. Once testing concludes and the results are as expected and aligned to the requirement, the production deployment can begin. If there is space server capacity, you can add a new container and then monitor the outcome. The document in the NoSQL database should contain different-looking values compared with the previous function version—for this container's output. The rest of the containers are still using the previous function version.

Once the production check for the container with the new function passes, full deployment occurs by destroying an old container and adding a new container. This process is then repeated until all the containers have the updated function. The change should be seamless to customers—with no interrupted transactions, the change was implemented without an outage, and no change was made to the database concerning the new value.

Yes, stateful code can be implemented in this manner; I intertwined stateless code and live deployment examples to maintain the scenario and the book flow.

Stateless SQL

Querying an Oracle table using the SELECT statement also represents stateless code because the data returned is not stored for use by future statements. To see the data again, the SQL statement has to be executed once more:

```
SELECT emp_id, emp_first_name, emp_last_name from employee where
emp_id = 10;
```

In contrast, using the SELECT INTO construct in which returned values are retained in variables represents stateful code:

```
SELECT emp_id, emp_first_name, emp_last_name INTO empid, empfirstname,
emplastname from employee where emp_id = 10;
```

The application can reference empid, empfirsname, and emplastname for further processing.

Stateless Web

Static Http pages are stateless; they are returned as-is upon request. When programmers add code to capture values or maintain session information, the Http pages become stateful. Using the hobbyist example already shown, a simple Http document that collects information from a person who wants to join the Hobbyist Guild needs the person's first and last name and at least one hobby (why join if you have no hobby?). Once the data is collected, the code derives the ID, maybe from a sequence generator, to complete the required values for insertion into a table or document. As guild membership expands, many of the most active hobbyists want to provide more information that can be shared between members—the first is an e-mail address.

The application code needs a few new lines to include a request for an e-mail address on the new member form. Using a NoSQL document database, the new data—e-mail address—can be included in the document within the same collection; no database change is required. For a relational database, the table has to be altered to add the new column before the data can be inserted. The same is true for updates. Existing hobbyists can add an e-mail address requiring a small amount of code on the update profile web page for the e-mail address entry. The e-mail address can be added to that person's document without defining a structure change. The relational table still requires the column to be added before the update occurs.

Stateless schemas should make much more sense now.

Relational databases with stateful schemas will not be completely replaced anytime soon because a need still exists for data to be captured in a relational model. Organizations have invested much time and effort into building and maintaining relational data stores. Relational databases continue to be single sources of truth for many critical data elements.

NoSQL databases serve a different purpose where availability and dynamic data collection is needed. Being able to add data to a document (record) without first having to define the new data element makes it possible to deploy code changes without database schema changes. DevOps teams (DBAs are team members) can focus on reducing cycle times, which gets software to market quickly. Decomposing monolithic applications and deconstructing portions of the relation data model expand the possibilities for Agile applications, stateless schemas and code while maintaining stateful data.

Summary

Stateless schemas and code undergird capabilities such as parallel code execution and dynamic data storage. NoSQL databases store data without predefined data types, accepting data that vary dramatically within a collection. Deploying changes to a production environment with little or no risk improves reliability while delivering new application functionality to customers. Parallel code execution accelerates application performance, which translates into improved customer experience. DevOps leverages these methods for improving application execution and deployment and for stabilizing infrastructure.

Finally, no matter what method, database, or process is leveraged to progress DevOps, remember that the data is stateful. Data integrity must be preserved.

Optimizing Application Performance with Change Management Improvements

Yes, the chapter title sounds intriguing—incomprehensible, but intriguing just the same. Application performance and change management seem to fit together like oil and water. For IT folks, the first thing that comes to mind when hearing *change management* is the ITIL ITSM process designed to minimize

© Michael S. Cuppett 2016

M. S. Cuppett, *DevOps, DBAs, and DBaaS*, DOI 10.1007/978-1-4842-2208-9_6

risks when changes are made to the production application environment. The change management process involves designing the change, testing the change, determining what impacts could occur, determining how the change can be backed out if it fails, testing the back-out, and then explaining the change and getting approval from the CAB to execute the change. A week has likely passed at this point, only to arrive at the place where the change is scheduled to occur. Change management must be accelerated to fit the DevOps methodology while keeping risk minimized. The DevOps approach requires extensive testing and the mandate to stop defects from progressing; the process is similar to workers on the manufacturing floor having the power to stop the line when problems occur that could impact safety or quality.

Optimizing application performance brings thoughts of code rewrites and database tuning to mind; change management usually does not make the to-do list for improving application performance. Instead, change management is a "mechanism" or "checkpoint" before the improvements are implemented into production. Viewed too often as an impediment, especially when a quick turnaround is needed, change management forces teams to assess changes and potential impacts to the production environment. Post–change production problems still occur too often, perhaps because change management occurs too late in the process and misses the discovery of nonproduction findings handled as issues without thought given to the same issue soon to be hampering production. When nonproduction and production environments are not exactly the same, it is easy for teams to consider issues to be relevant to a specific environment. No matter; the suitability of change management and application performance improvement is not obvious.

Melding application performance improvement and change management requires thinking about change management as more than simple risk management, covering everyone's butt, and a mere paperwork drill. How can value be mined from change management that can be applied toward improved application performance?

Change Analysis

Change analysis is the missing link. Not change analysis because something failed and the root cause needs to be determined—a process that still needs to exist, hopefully less frequently as DevOps takes hold—but rather assessing the performance impact of each change to understand where investments in performance improvements are making a difference for customers and the bottom line. Most changes are measured using a binary indicator: success or failure. That should be the starting point when implementing a change management process, but for many organizations it is also the ending point. Stopping there dramatically reduces the impact change management offers. Change analysis, which takes the premise of the chapter title at face value, appears to offer the opportunity for change management to optimize application performance. Data (the same type of data collected to analyze production performance problems) is needed for change analysis, but it is collected in each nonproduction instance prior to production to prevent performance problems making it to production.

Let's demonstrate change analysis using a theoretical internal application performance problem for a corporation. First, I will describe the problem and discuss how to get a handle on the true issue before getting to the analysis.

Call center representatives are reporting slowness when searching a customer's order history. The problem tickets record wait times in the range of 5 to 30 seconds. The infrastructure includes the user's desktop computer connected to the local area network (LAN) at 1Gbps, running an updated browser. The glass house environment hosts the virtual web, application, and database host tiers in a private cloud running a Linux OS and Oracle database as the primary transactional system. Additionally, the decision was made to maintain customer order history in a public cloud to keep the transactional database lean.

A web services call reaches out over a T3 45Mbps wide area network (WAN) to a cloud provider's data center that hosts the organization's data in a DBaaS solution involving the Linux OS hosting MongoDB (see Figure 6-1).

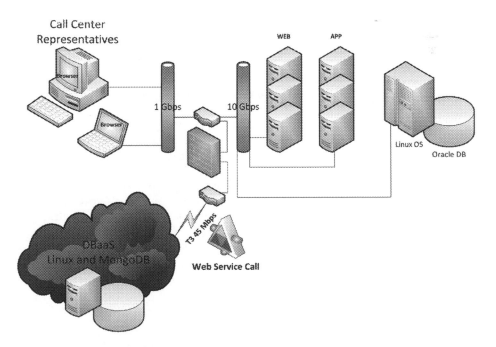

Figure 6-1. Example of an application infrastructure

The order history data pushed from the Oracle database tables is transformed into documents for an order history collection.

The application footprint, minus a small percentage of code for the web interface, is distributed 85–90% at the application tier; the remaining code is stored within the database as PLSQL packages, functions, triggers, and stored procedures. The web service call code is included with the code at the application layer, as shown in Figure 6-2.

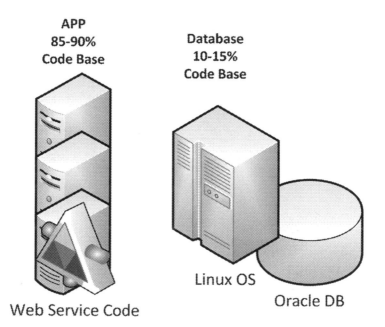

APP
85-90%
Code Base

Database
10-15%
Code Base

Web Service Code

Linux OS

Oracle DB

Figure 6-2. Example of an application code distribution

Understanding User-Reported Problems

The challenge with user–reported application slowness is the subjectivity of each person's perception of time. What feels like 10 seconds to one person may feel like 30 seconds to a less patient person like me. I have to admit that waiting more than a few seconds for a response from anything on the Internet makes me want to check the news to find out whether the Internet is down. Yes, the whole Internet. Some users make the effort to get a wall clock time of the wait, but that also does not provide the accuracy needed. Without totally disregarding the user's subjectivity (because obviously there is a problem), getting objective data is key to understanding the user experience.

Objective Timings

There are many ways to collect detailed information for capturing exact timings from a user perspective. If possible, test from several workstations of users who are experiencing the problem and several workstations for users who are not experiencing the problem, given that each is doing similar work. If possible, test from your workstation or other location workstations. If a problem exists, the users need to know that you understand their concerns—showing empathy goes a long way toward good will, which is something IT teams need desperately. Sitting with users or talking on the phone with users while remotely accessing the computer makes a more personal connection; emailing or texting misses this important customer service opportunity. Remember, DevOps is about understanding the business and working with the business team more closely, so verbal communications are critical.

End-to-End Response Time

Network packet collectors such as Netmon or Wireshark capture network traffic and provide information about when a request was sent until the response was received—from the network perspective as the capture is taken at the computer's network interface. The gap is the presentation layer, the processing that happens between the browser and the network on the computer. For that, using a product such as Fiddler, HttpWatch, or the Inspect function in certain browsers provide the truest timings.

Combining a packet capture and a browser-level timing makes determining slowness on the user's computer relatively easy, although only a very minute percentage of application performance problems happen at the local computer. But just because multiple users have reported slowness, you should not disregard the client infrastructure. Many companies distribute the same image to many computers, which allows for the possibility that a client-side change has caused a problem. Figure 6-3 demonstrates a packet capture, showing packet sequence, time elements, and packet descriptions.

Frame Number	Time Date Local Adjusted	Time Offset	Description
647	7:44:23 PM 9/12/2016	1.0950777	TCP:Flags=...A..S., SrcPort=HTTP Alternate(8080),
648	7:44:23 PM 9/12/2016	1.0953387	TCP:Flags=...A...., SrcPort=51312, DstPort=HTTP .
649	7:44:23 PM 9/12/2016	1.0957022	HTTP:Request, CONNECT www.oracle.com:443
650	7:44:23 PM 9/12/2016	1.0963560	HTTP:Request, CONNECT www.oracle.com:443
651	7:44:23 PM 9/12/2016	1.0965210	TCP:Flags=...A..S., SrcPort=HTTP Alternate(8080),
652	7:44:23 PM 9/12/2016	1.0967866	TCP:Flags=...A...., SrcPort=51313, DstPort=HTTP .
653	7:44:23 PM 9/12/2016	1.0973894	HTTP:Request, CONNECT www.oracleimg.com:443
656	7:44:23 PM 9/12/2016	1.0992365	TCP:Flags=...A..S., SrcPort=HTTP Alternate(8080),
657	7:44:23 PM 9/12/2016	1.0995025	TCP:Flags=...A...., SrcPort=51314, DstPort=HTTP .
659	7:44:23 PM 9/12/2016	1.1001835	TCP:Flags=...A..S., SrcPort=HTTP Alternate(8080),
662	7:44:23 PM 9/12/2016	1.1009446	TCP:Flags=...A...., SrcPort=51315, DstPort=HTTP .
663	7:44:23 PM 9/12/2016	1.1012075	TCP:Flags=...A..S., SrcPort=HTTP Alternate(8080),
664	7:44:23 PM 9/12/2016	1.1015059	TCP:Flags=...A..S., SrcPort=HTTP Alternate(8080),
665	7:44:23 PM 9/12/2016	1.1018612	TCP:Flags=...A...., SrcPort=51317, DstPort=HTTP .
666	7:44:23 PM 9/12/2016	1.1018924	TCP:Flags=...A...., SrcPort=51318, DstPort=HTTP .
667	7:44:23 PM 9/12/2016	1.1021308	TCP:Flags=...A..S., SrcPort=HTTP Alternate(8080),
668	7:44:23 PM 9/12/2016	1.1022591	TCP:Flags=...A...., SrcPort=51316, DstPort=HTTP .
669	7:44:23 PM 9/12/2016	1.1029645	HTTP:Request, CONNECT www.oracleimg.com:443
670	7:44:23 PM 9/12/2016	1.1032578	HTTP:Request, CONNECT www.oracleimg.com:443

Figure 6-3. Example of a network packet capture

▓ **Note** The packet capture can be analyzed further to determine transaction times (a process not covered in this book).

Figure 6-4 shows a proxy capture using HttpWatch. Notice the http calls, execution duration bars, and time data.

Started	Time Chart	! ▶	Time	Sent	Received	Method	Result
▣ 00:00:00.000	Oracle	Integrated Cloud Applications and Platform Services						
+0.000		!	0.004	0	0	GET	(Cache)
+0.004		!	0.011	0	0	GET	(Cache)
+0.021		!	0.002	0	0	GET	(Cache)
+0.025		!	0.001	0	0	GET	(Cache)
+0.028		!	0.001	0	0	GET	(Cache)
+0.030	▬▬▬▬▬▬		1.201	437	1386	GET	200
+0.032		!	0.002	0	0	GET	(Cache)
+0.172	▬▬▬▬▬▬▬▬	!	1.954	501	2705	GET	403
+0.178		!	0.002	0	0	GET	(Cache)
+0.181		!	0.001	0	0	GET	(Cache)
+0.198			0.001	0	0	GET	(Cache)
+0.202	▬▬▬▬	!	0.798	389	3338	GET	403
+0.205	▬▬▬▬▬	!	1.173	421	682	GET	200
+0.208		!	0.001	0	0	GET	(Cache)
+0.223		!	0.001	0	0	GET	(Cache)

Figure 6-4. Example of an HttpWatch browser proxy capture

The duration bars make it easy to see which calls take the most time. Imagine the example data being from your application with timings ten times as high. Improving application performance with just this information is possible by investigating each long bar http call.

Figure 6-5 was captured using the browser's Inspect tool, which is accessed by right-clicking the web page in a location without links (a blank space).

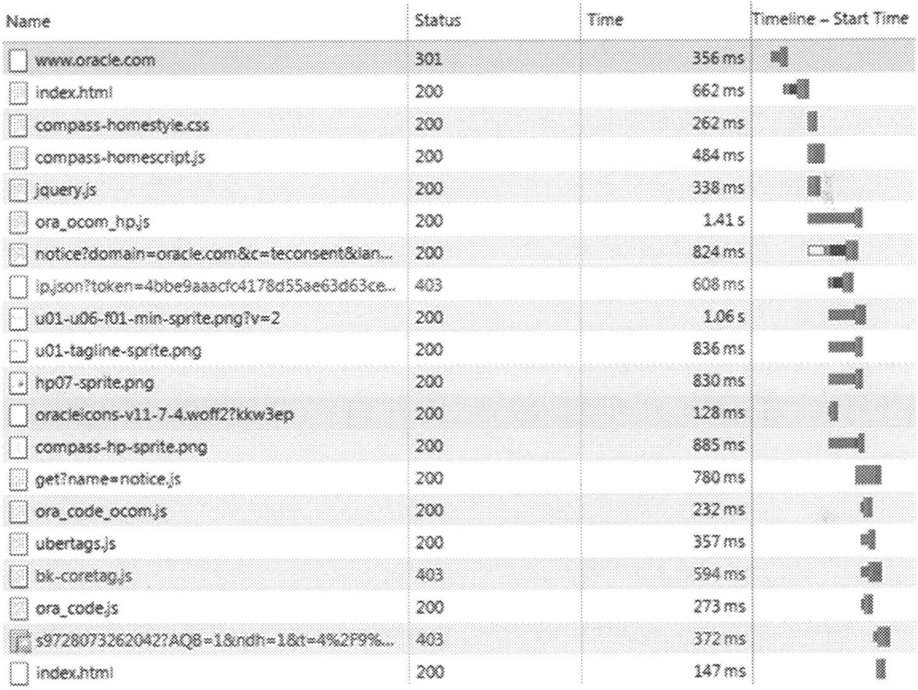

Name	Status	Time	Timeline – Start Time
www.oracle.com	301	356 ms	
index.html	200	662 ms	
compass-homestyle.css	200	262 ms	
compass-homescript.js	200	484 ms	
jquery.js	200	338 ms	
ora_ocom_hp.js	200	1.41 s	
notice?domain=oracle.com&c=teconsent&lan...	200	824 ms	
ip.json?token=4bbe9aaacfc4178d55ae63d63ce...	403	608 ms	
u01-u06-f01-min-sprite.png?v=2	200	1.06 s	
u01-tagline-sprite.png	200	836 ms	
hp07-sprite.png	200	830 ms	
oracleicons-v11-7-4.woff2?kkw3ep	200	128 ms	
compass-hp-sprite.png	200	885 ms	
get?name=notice.js	200	780 ms	
ora_code_ocom.js	200	232 ms	
ubertags.js	200	357 ms	
bk-coretag.js	403	594 ms	
ora_code.js	200	273 ms	
s9728073262042?AQ8=1&ndh=1&t=4%2F9%...	403	372 ms	
index.html	200	147 ms	

Figure 6-5. Example of a browser Inspect capture

Note Again, the long statement durations have to be investigated further for potential performance enhancements.

Similar analysis should be done as part of the DevOps pipeline to hunt and kill performance-draining beasts. As code is tested in the pipeline against the development and integration ecosystems, collecting performance data sets enables a deep analysis of each code statement's impact on performance. Obviously, statements found violating predetermined baseline performance values must be tuned prior to production release.

Although I simply collected data using a browser call to www.oracle.com to provide simple examples, code performance analysis may require including code within the application that captures performance information or start and stop times for each execution. By now, you may realize that the types and count of the possible checks are vast; your goal is to determine which checks, done where, bring the best results. The infrastructure example exists in real life because customers visiting the company web site expect great response times. What happens behind the curtain is the DevOps team's responsibility to deliver. If the application reaches out for credit card authorization or to validate the visitor's membership needed for a discount, that time needs to be analyzed before and after changes are made.

As shown, digging out exact timings provides a much better understanding of the application performance—broken into manageable chunks for analysis and correction.

Yes, There Really Is a Problem

It is not that we do not believe user-reported information; it is just that experience tells us that other factors can be in play that make it necessary to get the full representation of the problem. One user would complain several times a week about application slowness, which was causing the person's performance metrics to drop. Upon investigation using a packet capture tool, it was determined that the live video streaming to the user's computer was causing the application slowness. This person was advised to stop the streaming and given the heads up that the company could "see" everything. Nothing illegal was happening, but complaining about self-inflicted impaired performance caused by news/entertainment traffic does not boost careers if that information is shared.

Continuing with our hypothetical problem: the user-side investigations recorded slowness consistently in the 5–17 seconds range, with very few outliers, which narrows the actual slowness impact significantly. If you are lucky, the captures you already have point to a single call that represents the majority of the slowness, allowing immediate focus on what is likely the root cause.

As member of a DevOps IT shop, you know that software releases occur nightly. Unfortunately, the users did not report the problem immediately, making it difficult to establish when the problem was introduced, (except that everything seemed to be good a few weeks ago; and, by the way, the problem occurs at different times of the day; otherwise, performance is acceptable). The release report shows at least five changes that may have impacted this functionality: four were implemented successfully, and one had to be rolled back with no root cause documented. Here, the binary release check has failed the organization. Release success or failure does not communicate information

needed by the business or IT. Code that is successfully deployed with functionality validated by a tester does not tell the entire story (for example, performance degradation being introduced). DevOps testing purposely initiates
more comprehensive answers. Excessive testing vets the software thoroughly
and automatically, making it feasible to include tests designed to measure performance. It gives the green light only on performance that matches or is
faster than a predefined value or the previous code version timing.

As DevOps teams "shift-left" and work in conjunction with business leaders as product managers, IT (now DevOps) truly becomes partners with the
business. The "IT alignment to the business" goal included in the annual IT
strategy deck for the last decade becomes obsolete. The perceived (or actual)
misalignment was not only because the business teams did not understand
what IT really did, other than spending offensively huge chunks of money
to drive business operations, IT also wholly failed to come to the table as a
business partner; instead remaining aloof and detached from everything but
technology.

Thirty years ago, IT, MIS, or data processing (whatever the name) was given
the mission of finding ways to complete work faster than teams of people
could by having computers do mundane, repeatable tasks. Ironically, DevOps
in many ways reaches back 40 years to repeat the tactical execution of having computers do mundane tasks: repetitive code testing, deployments, infrastructure as code, and more. Between then and now, far too many manual
steps were added to processes that now need to be remediated. Forty years
ago, computer work likely resulted in teams of people losing their jobs, but
DevOps does not have the same mandate as in the data processing years.
Instead, highly skilled engineers and programmers are freed from repetitive
tasks and allowed to partner with the business to generate and implement
game-changing technologies and applications.

DevOps wants and needs to shift talented, intelligent, experienced staff into
roles that deliver measurable benefits for the company. Repeatable tasks can
be done much faster by computers, but computers do not generate ideas.
Computers running data analytics programs churn through data millions of
times faster than humans, but computers still do not have the capability to
find answers in the data, interpret the data, or act on the data like people do.
People assimilate varying data points to produce value in new ways. DevOps
needs people to create opportunities to help the business leapfrog competi-
tors. It is not intended to get rid of people; instead, it wants to make people
more effective and focused on executing business strategies, not hampered by
mundane tasks. Accomplishments have moved from "Designed a new algorithm
for …" to "Improved customer experience … reduced costs … implemented
a new revenue channel …"

DBAs and DevOps teams should take a positive stance and attitude toward
the goals of Agile and DevOps, knowing that each person's impact on the

organization can make tremendous strides to create better customer experiences and software products, and continually improve business processes, all with prospective top- and bottom-line impacts.

DevOps Answers

Change management analysis in DevOps extends beyond binary conclusions to business impact statements. Reporting successful or failed statuses alone shifts to informative, customer-centric statuses such as the following:

- "Change 123 implementing function A successfully reduced execution time 40%; now averaging 7 milliseconds per call."

- "The change to reorganize table ABC successfully reduced report execution time, allowing the business to meet contractual requirements."

- "Change 456 failed and was rolled over successfully with change 512. Testing for change 456 did not include a critical data test; later found and tested for change 512, which allowed the failure to advance. Teams had rectified, tested, and implemented the needed test earlier this week, having change 512 already in the pipeline. The 512 push completed successfully within the change window, eliminating the risk."

DevOps' fail fast edict can really benefit the company by progressing software products continuously and without having laborious rollbacks, rework, retests, and reimplementation. In the previous third scenario, the DevOps team knows that a communication was missed because change 456 should have never made it to the release stage, let alone production.

So as change management communications pivot from mundane status updates to business impact updates, opportunities to improve application performance become more apparent. Moving from a message that the code was implemented successfully to a message that the code decreased customer query time by 67% tells a better story. There is a large chasm between code that works and code that works and executes expectantly fast while generating an audit trail. Adding a new feature that performs poorly is not really a feature—it is a bug and a frustration for customers. Adding a feature that is expected to increase mobile app usage 400% without increasing infrastructure resources is not a feature, but a colossal failure. The DevOps movement provides the needed tactical response with infrastructure as code. When traffic is expected to spike, adding resources to existing virtual hosts or spinning up additional hosts with a button click or two simplifies infrastructure readiness and resiliency.

Performance Isolation

Several previous examples showed end-to-end, customer experience transactional times. Next, timings need to be gathered for each tier involved in the processing of the order history transaction. It is expected that the findings correlate with the end-to-end times: 5–17 seconds, minus outliers. Timings for workstation to web server, web server to app server, app server to database server, and the web service processing time provide clear transaction breakpoints. Look at the data in Table 6-1.

Table 6-1. Example Performance Data at Transaction Breakpoints

Response Times (in Milliseconds)	Test 1	Test 2	Test 3	Test 4	Avg.	
Client to Web	21	34	27	31	28.25	
Web to App	62	54	87	68	67.75	
App to DB	3763	3841	4639	2049	3573	a
API Call	5218	2567	9497	2817	5024.75	b
Total:	9064	6496	14250	4965	8693.75	c

Immediately, two parts of the transaction register as extremely slow, with the average execution times shown by a and b. All four tests had total execution times within the 5–17 second range, with the average time shown at c. Ignoring the client-to-web-to-app segments and discovering the root cause for the slow execution times from the app server to the database server and for the API call should lead to significant decreases in response time.

DBAs can execute session traces to find which SQL statements are involved and how long each statement takes to return the result set. In this case, the excessive time is being spent in the database, caused by the query having to do a full table scan of the order table to get the order numbers to be pulled from the order history collection. A trigger is also in place that writes an audit record to a table that shows high insert contention. The DevOps team agrees that an index is needed for the order table and that the audit table contention, although not good, is not critical enough to address right now because the contention accounts for only a few milliseconds. The contention issue is not a priority in the backlog. The index add is a priority fix to be implemented immediately after testing, bypassing the standard backlog process.

A DBA writes the `Create Index` statement and checks the code into the repository for the CI server to incorporate into the main code branch and to test. In parallel, a developer punches out a new test that would specifically execute the query with the new index, reporting the execution time in an e-mail to the entire DevOps team. The e-mailed results show an average execution time of less than 100 milliseconds; the team then releases the code for deployment. After the deployment, the product manager reaches out to a subset of the users who reported the problem, with feedback similar to "It seems faster, but it is still too slow." Understanding that less than 50% of the transaction time has been addressed so far, the team begins to investigate the API call slowness. The cloud provider's hourly transaction time report consistently shows response times under 300 milliseconds, leaving the network in question. Initial checks show excellent round-trip response times.

Leaving only the WAN segment as the possible culprit, the DevOps team requests that the network team monitor the WAN. After several days, the network team reports that three times daily, at different times, a large volume of data was sent from the Oracle database server to the cloud provider, resulting in substantial packet losses, retransmissions, and connection timeouts. The teams quickly conclude that the job responsible for uploading order history data could be causing the problem. Comparing the network saturation times with user reported slowness times confirms a correlation within the business day. Network saturations during the night did not conflict with user transactions. Further investigation found that the upload jobs were not running at the same time daily, as planned a year prior during the implementation. Instead of the job starting at a specific time during the night, the job start time was being set to when the job completed, causing the start time to drift until eventually running during the business day. Separately, what was supposed to be a single daily upload turned into three daily uploads. The upload job was inadvertently scheduled three times, and each job loaded the same data set for the day because record selection included all records older than 180 days. To complicate things further, the same job was failing to remove the order history records, causing the upload record count to increase daily. Further investigation revealed that the MongoDB database had significant numbers of duplicate records.

The DevOps team developed a plan to first empty the MongoDB database, followed by uploading all the order history records in scope, purging the same records from the Oracle database, fixing the job code to make sure that records are deleted daily, and finally removing two of three scheduled jobs. The much smaller data set being uploaded during the night resulted in the user reporting excellent application performance, better than ever. It turns out that the upload issue pushed users past what they were willing to consider acceptable application performance: less than 5 seconds. Additional response time improvement came from the Oracle query fix that was responsible for the preupload problem average times of nearly 5 seconds. With both issues resolved, response times were subsecond.

The two changes that made application usage very acceptable for the users could be reported as successful or a failure, except now you know that the change management report needs to include details about how the change made an impact on the users and the business. Not recording the benefits in the change record seems irresponsible in light of DevOps practices.

Maturing change management from infancy with the limited vocabulary of success or fail evolves change management into a business-empowering function. DevOps speeds change delivery, but only after excessive testing that is purposed to not allow defects to proceed. It is important to note that change management must shift-left several steps from being a production release process to become a milestone starting at code check-in through deployments; change management is not a production-only tool. Changes identified as successful by developers testing on their workstations must include performance considerations, which must be rectified as needed before being introduced into the full product code base. Additionally, CI testing must include load and stress testing to ensure that the code performs just as quickly when competing with peak load times during the business day.

Manually troubleshooting a performance problem is time-consuming, as demonstrated here. Investments in APM or similar tools with different acronyms set the business up with the capability to proactively monitor applications, allowing performance corrections to be implemented before users are impacted. Reacting to real-time performance trends sure beats reacting to user complaints.

Change management seems an unlikely candidate for application performance improvement. DevOps again dispels the status quo by morphing a dreaded paperwork exercise into an effective communications tool. Reporting business improvements to customer experience or company financials, the DevOps team becomes a business partner known for speed to market, agility, and the willingness to accept business changes as routine, not scope-expanding challenges. Establishing DevOps principles as the cultural norm shifts the business' perception of IT, which is a much-needed good thing.

Summary

Change management to improve application performance can be done, as demonstrated in this chapter. Two significant shifts must occur. First, change management has to move backward from production implementations to all implementations as the code and database changes progress the pipeline. Second, purposeful performance data collections need to undergo a thorough analysis to disallow performance degrading changes to progress. DevOps advocates not allowing defects to progress, insisting on immediate mitigation. DBAs and DevOps teams need to consider performance killers as defects requiring immediate remediation.

Measuring DBA Inputs to End-User Experience and Business Value

People want to be recognized for work well done; it is just human nature. The challenge for IT folks is being able to quantify how application, infrastructure, and operational changes improve the business by making customers happier, leaning processes, or contributing to revenue increases or cost decreases. Cumulative degradation mathematically reveals what IT leaders have struggled against when defining metrics to prove IT's value to the business (refer to Table 1-1 in Chapter 1). Imagine the CIO sharing uptime metrics with other CXOs, knowing that the CXOs are hearing daily from their teams that the application systems are unstable and slow. A CIO stating 99.9% uptime undoubtedly

© Michael S. Cuppett 2016
M. S. Cuppett, *DevOps, DBAs, and DBaaS*, DOI 10.1007/978-1-4842-2208-9_7

receives flak from the other chiefs. *Uptime*, which means that the computer is running and the application works, is much different from a measure showing productive use of the application to meet business and consumer demands.

The trick is converting technical outcomes into financial or customer benefit measurements. For each of the examples in this chapter, take time to consider how to communicate the value message. For example, reducing overall database server load may delay capital outlay or reduce monthly DBaaS costs. Decreasing transaction times leads to improved customer satisfaction, which may be reflected in the company's net promoter score, reduced complaints, or increased revenue. Transform the technical measure into financial- or customer-impacting news.

Customer Experience

Time is everything for IT when measuring customer experience, which cumulative degradation does not measure. Cumulative degradation does not account for transaction times, which is the determinate that customers observe. Marketing analyzes the number of clicks to purchase, cross-selling, conversions, and more under the customer experience management (CEM) umbrella. Marketing manages the unique needs of customers, while IT needs to make sure transactions are fast! All marketing metrics suffer when transaction performance degrades: response times lengthen and the expectations of every unique customer are not met. Although it may not be intuitive to see how clicks to purchase and cross-selling are impacted by performance, consider the likelihood of customer abandonment. Customers can become impatient and discard slow transactions, quickly jumping to competitor sites or waiting to try again in the future.

Although systems performing poorly are technically "up" or "available," customer frustration reveals a different sentiment. Applications not performing to the service level agreement (SLA) or to other expectations should be labeled degraded. When performance worsens, the applications should be considered unavailable. Patience is a virtue, but it is a character attribute not exercised by most people who are waiting for an application to respond.

Fortunately, the industry has recognized this disconnect and has moved to customer experience—internal and external—as a measure of application delivery success. Online retailers design infrastructure and applications with the intent that a customer never leaves the site due to application unresponsiveness. The goal is to deliver an experience in which the customer finds, reviews, decides, and purchases items quickly and effortlessly. Beyond performance, cumbersome navigation, slowness, or ambiguous checkout form fields can also drive customers to competing sites. Now that DBAs are DevOps team members, issues such as navigation and poorly performing web forms become areas of concern because each team member is responsible for every component contributing to the product. The opportunity to push responsibility to another team—finger pointing—does not exist in Agile and DevOps.

DBAs need to contribute and report contributions to customer experience improvements. Measuring customer experience by using the cumulative model provides paths forward in determining where to invest time, money, and people. Upping the availability for any segment decreases degradation, leading to improved customer experience. DBA participation traditionally involved database tuning first, operating OSs and storage improvements second, and the full IT supply chain serving the application third.

Measuring customer experience by transaction times tells a better story. Delivering 99% of transactions at 10 seconds versus delivering 95% of transactions at 1 second are two very different customer experience stories. All 99% of the transactions in the first scenario reflect a poor customer experience when matched against the industry standard of 3 seconds. The second scenario represents excellent customer experience from very fast response times, but the caveat is that 5% of the transactions were too slow, which is an unacceptable number. For both, unavailability is never good, but my observations show that customers are more gracious when a site is not available—they know that problems can occur—than they are when a site is slow. As mentioned before, it may be a wiser move to take a site down to perform a fix rather than trying to push through the performance problem. When the site is available, the site needs to perform excellently to maintain acceptable customer experience levels.

Good News: DevOps and Virtualization

The very good news comes in two flavors, DevOps and virtualization, which are tremendously exciting options for addressing performance degradation. Dynamic resource management is one reason why virtualization became popular. Adding CPU or memory to a struggling guest provides a quick and easy solution for performance problems, at least in many cases. Depending on the database and version, improved performance depends on the database implementation being able to dynamically consume additional resources. If the database supports dynamic memory expansion, the database should be able to consume an additional memory outlay.

As explained here, DevOps presents the opportunity to spin up additional servers to increase capacity, especially at the application tier. Templates can be used to build servers for new projects or to build servers to expand capacity to resolve performance challenges.

Application and infrastructure play different roles, depending on where your customer is in the application process. The application presentation and functionality in which customers step through different selections is driven more by the application than the infrastructure. In contrast, once a customer initiates a transaction, infrastructure delivery capability increases in importance.

Customer experience during screen navigation depends on the compute environment (phone, tablet, laptop, kiosk, etc.) and the client–side interface application code. If the application makes frequent service calls to back-end systems to populate fields as the consumer progresses through the screen, the infrastructure contributes to the experience—good or bad. For demonstration purposes, let's have the application be a simple registration form with no back-end calls. The user experience depends on the application flow from one input field to the next and to the user's smartphone or computer. User frustration might come from unexampled data entry formatting, but it is not likely relative to performance. Once the user clicks Submit, response time becomes everything, making the infrastructure and database germane to the customer experience. As newly anointed DevOps team members, DBAs must ensure that the customer data inserts quickly and securely into the database, and must work with other infrastructure teams to drive network and server speediness.

First, it is necessary to measure customer experience holistically and at each technical entrance-exit to understand which technologies impact customer experience.

Holistic End-User Experience

Pulling together a quick list of technologies that contribute to the customer experience is not as simple as it sounds. Network, web, app, and database servers come to mind quickly; then authentication for secure access, and, of course, the customer compute platform. What about transaction auditing, acquiring a security certificate, encryption, proxies or reverse proxies, DNS, load balancers, secure connectivity, firewalls, security scans, and more? Depending on the architectural complexity, much more could be added to this list. Oh, I almost forgot the application code, which could include client-side, web, app, and database code. The application may hook into the phone system or offer a live-chat feature, all impacting experience and performance, good or bad.

During a recent client engagement—a disaster recovery exercise—dependencies continued to be revealed during the exercise, even after months of preparation with application, infrastructure, and architecture teams. Systems are complex, uniquely built, and supported by silo-ed teams, making sure that no one fully grasps the environment. Plan, build, run organizations divide work, which impedes understanding. People designing the system likely never see the end product or may not recognize the end solution. Application builds require thought continuity, ensuring that design drives the build and the build runs sustainably.

DevOps marries a plethora of skilled engineers into a team that together knows every piece and part of the system, all reinforced by cross-working born from skill overlap. Extreme programming generates code faster and cleaner by using two developers working in tandem and providing each other with ideas, syntax checks, and alternative coding techniques from past experiences.

DevOps team blending provides comparable wins, reinforced through team knowledge sharing, and transference to new team members when needed. Single point-of-failure staffers are detrimental to organizational resiliency, yet they exist more than is admitted. When projects have to pause because an engineer leaves the company, it indicates that knowledge gaps exist relative to the application or technology served by the lost team member.

"See" the Application Ecosystem

Reviewing an application architecture or infrastructure diagram, such as the one shown in Figure 7-1, and intending to identify every technology involved and the contribution of each to response time can be telling and challenging.

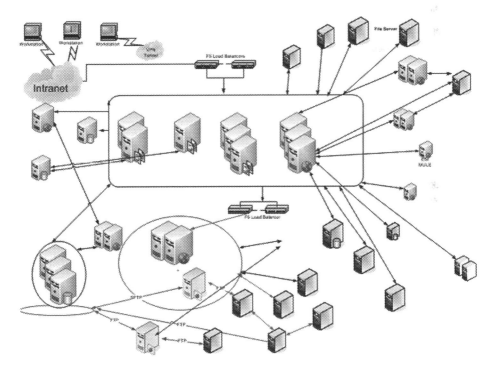

Figure 7-1. Core application with extensive integration dependencies

Although a senior IT engineer friend of mine does a great job keeping the (scrubbed by author) document updated, when she shares the diagram, she still deliberately qualifies that the architecture shows the known environment because she has been enlightened to many additional puzzle pieces during overnight triage calls. She expects additional findings.

Too many of us have experienced long triage calls in which everything seems to be okay, but the system is failing. Then a voice interrupts the call, saying, "You know, about 3 years ago we implemented code that was supposed to send e-mail to people, but it never worked. But we left the code in place because the failure occurred very quickly and did not impact the users." After a few more hours of investigation, it is determined that the e-mail server the "broken" code was reaching out to had been shut down in preparation for decommissioning. The result: the failing code that had been able to reach and fail in 20 milliseconds extended to 2 minutes when the e-mail server was downed—the 2-minute mark was a timeout that was reached.

Real-time Application Monitoring

Match what was learned about the ecosystem with real-time data from an APM tool or a combination of network packet captures, application logs, and database traces, and the intricate details start being exposed. If you have ever wondered why "the application is slow" triages take time, the answer lies in finding the performance outlier (or outliers) across a complex environment that accounts for the time causing the degradation. Server or database crashes, down network segments, or failed authentication servers do not require 40-person triage calls. Properly positioned monitoring, logging, and synthetic transactions ease and shorten triage time, yet still retard achieving optimal performance, availability, and reliability.

Metrics must be defined thoroughly and explicitly, including start and finish points. Define this SLA statement: "Every database transaction must complete in less than .5 seconds." DBAs might reason that the database must complete each call in one-half second, the start time is when the call gets to the database, and the stop time is when the result set exits the database. A call center associate likely expects the half second to cover the time starting with Submit until the screen refresh. Definitive verbiage rectifies this disparity.

Measures that Matter

Submit to screen refresh that is broken down by transaction function or type demonstrates the end-user perspective. This data gathering could be done with a stopwatch, but additional accuracy is gained with browser metrics or proxy tool metrics, as explained in Chapter 6.

Knowing the total average time for different transactions starts the metrics communications and trending processes. Discerning where each time segment—milliseconds to minutes—specifically occurs divides the transaction into investigable pieces (see Figure 7-2) that equal the total transaction time when summed.

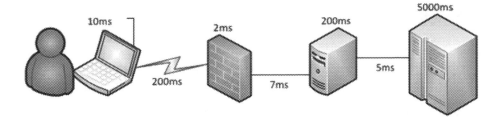

Figure 7-2. Simple transaction time breakdown across the infrastructure

Once the transaction has been divided, look for low-hanging fruit, such as a 5-second slot from when the transaction enters the database server until it departs the database server. Five seconds is a significant chunk of time on a database server, especially if it represents the majority of the total transaction time.

Further measures are needed to determine how the 5 seconds accumulates on the server. Once on the server, determining database time is key. If the database time represents most of the 5 seconds, more digging should lead to an outlier: long storage read time, a full scan of an object that needs an index, an implicit data conversion, or a bad execution plan.

Correcting the slowness and reducing the 5 seconds to .5 seconds is a win that senior management needs to hear about to know that the DevOps team makes a difference for the customer and company.

Pivoting from triage impact to DevOps impact calls for a perspective change. As DBAs get closer to the design phase, opportunities to prevent issues and to instill best practices are presented. As mentioned in Chapter 2, some DBAs historically have made the effort to find out what changes or new functionality are in the software build pipeline. If the DevOps team includes this DBA type, the pivot is not of concern. For DBAs that, by choice or organizational culture, do not become aware of changes until it is really too late to alter the design, this pivot is essential.

DevOps' mandate to not allow failures to progress, including performance non-conformers, swings the problem finding and resolution efforts away from production. Being okay with a few functional tests, a small regression, and no stress or load testing is no longer an acceptable practice. When reading or discussing Agile, you see that the code first, build test sequence is reversed. Building a test to validate that the business function requirement is met before coding is a common recommendation. Additionally, a slew of other automated tests should be used to basically ensure that no defect could ever occur. If a defect ever does make it into production, tests are built immediately to stop reoccurrence and are applied to as many other products as possible. Shared learning across products is encouraged.

Think about the pivot as moving all the effort used to triage problems in production to proactively preventing problems from being released into production.

Optimal

Supply chains, manufacturing processes, and end-to-end application transactions all have optimal timings. *Optimal*, defined as the fastest sustainable run time, scores high points on the efficiency scale. A knowledge of the capability of each component involved in the process aligns expectations. A five-step manufacturing process involving machines with different throughputs cannot be expected to produce products based on the machine with the highest throughput rating. Figure 7-3 displays five "machines" operating sequentially with defined maximum throughput ratings.

5-step Manufacturing Process

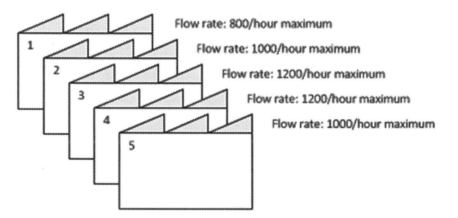

Figure 7-3. Manufacturing process example

As shown in Figure 7-3, the maximum throughput for the 5-step process is 800 units per hour, the rating of machine 1. The other four machines have to be dialed back to not to starve for work. The maximum rate, although achievable, is usually not the sustainable rate. If 700 units per hour for machine 1 is the recommended rate (100 less than maximum), the productivity loss on the other four machines is significant. If sales are good and there is a demand for more product more quickly, replacing machine 1 with a machine capable of 1,000 units per hour makes sense. To go higher than 1,000 units per hour is not warranted because machines 2 and 5 cannot support the higher output level. The new sustainable rate of 900 units per hour boosts production by more than 25%. To go higher, the three 1,000-units-per-hour machines would have to be replaced with 1,200-units-per-hour machines, upping the output to 1,100 units per hour.

Cumulative Degradation

Table 1-1 in Chapter 1 showed the impact of cumulative degradation. Using that data, investments to improve app server and database availability should provide the highest ROI. For instance, Table 7-1 shows the app server and database being improved to 99%, bringing the customer experience to 96.23%.

Table 7-1. Cumulative Degradation After Investment

Component	Success %
Network	99.9%
Web Server	99.7%
App Server	99%
Database	99%
App Server	99%
Web Server	99.7%
Network	99.9%

Customer Experience: 96.23%

Jumping from 92.41% to 96.23% should reduce the number of complaints received. Incremental improvements moving the needle from the middle 90s to the high 90s are reasonable investments; moving beyond 99% gets extremely pricey.

Optimal processing may be a percentage of the lowest throughput value because feeding and caring can reduce total throughput. Optimization stems from long run times interrupted only for required maintenance. For instance, a drink can–filling operation is optimized when cans are filled constantly from line startup, after the last cleaning or maintenance, until the line must be shut down for the next cleaning or maintenance. Short-run products must provide a margin high enough to cover the indirect costs of line changes, cleaning, and missed opportunity for other products. One client could run several products flat out for days, stopping only for mandated cleaning or product exhaustion. Inversely, the client would also stop long product runs for short-run stock keeping units (SKUs). Not only did the short runs stop efficient product runs but they also required 8 hours of line change work and cleaning before and after. The product sold at a premium, which covered the direct costs of materials and production expenses, but with the 16 hours of cutover labor and lost productivity—16 hours of no product being produced on that line—the product was being sold at a net loss. Companies sell products at a loss to gain good will, new customers, and for other strategic reasons, but without these possibilities, losing money on a product must end. The client stopped producing the short-run product on demand, choosing to limit production to longer runs with associated marketing campaigns to increase customer desire for the "special run" product.

Application throughput also has a calculable minimal processing time. Each hop across the infrastructure adds time; ignoring that truth does not mitigate the performance impact. Balancing architecture design to performance impact challenges everyone; being aware of the need to do so is a head start. Public DBaaS solutions come with inherent network latency, making application tier placement a critical decision because most multitier solutions transport more data between the database and app tier (in contrast with all other infrastructure hops).

Network latency must be applied to each packet. For a 20-millisecond network hop, 5 network packets containing database data would transfer in 100 milliseconds. Many database payloads require more than five packets. The amount of data being transferred directly impacts transaction duration.

Simply Overlooked

When complexity is an understated description of the application ecosystem, foundational or simple troubleshooting techniques are overlooked in lieu of the search for complicated problems or a reaction to past events directing where to seek fault.

A few years ago, when I was working as an Oracle DBA, an application slowness issue showed up: the application users were complaining about screen changes consistently taking 5 to 6 seconds. Of course, the database was the initial suspect, but fortunately it was easy enough to prove that the database was responding very quickly and that the performance trends had not spiked or dropped. The business had taken action with notable adverse consequences. First, they told the call center associates to track call details in Word when speaking with customers. Once finished with the call, the associates were to make themselves unavailable for calls long enough to enter the data into the application. From the customer's perspective, calls took about the same time as before the slowness was introduced. From a productivity perspective, it was unfortunate. Not only was it slow entering that data into the application but the impact also now included recording the details in Word—a double whammy!

In the end, the root cause was a 500-millisecond delay at the app server's network interface card (NIC). Five to 6 seconds of delays required only 10–12 packets to process through the NIC. By simply pinging the loopback address (127.0.0.1) and then the router to corroborate the timing (it was hard to believe), the problem was discovered. Aligned to an initiative to move from physical to virtual servers, an engineer performed a physical-to-virtual (P2V) migration that resolved the problem. Never forget the simple.

RRPs/IRP

Rapid response plans (RRPs) and/or incident response plans (IRPs) are great troubleshooting process documents. The idea is for each team in a silo-ed IT shop or for the DevOps team to be able to access infrastructure health rapidly—15 to 20 minutes, tops. Whether executed manually, with automation, or in a combination, the purpose was to isolate root cause or eliminate 95% or more of the infrastructure as not being contributors to the problem. Extensive monitoring and APM tools reduce the effort and bring a proactive posture to operations.

Preplanning how to respond to failures or performance degradations minimizes triage time, increasing system availability. All the effort and people-hour costs to build RRPs or IRPs pay for themselves after just a few calls that last one-half or one-quarter of the time of earlier average triage call durations.

The Fix Should Not Cost More Than the Problem

Network packet size can be modified to reduce the total packets needed, but that leads to other concerns that may create unmanageable maintenance tasks. Unless you are working with a private network link that is specific to multidatabase replication, network packet size changes offer little benefit. Having to invest more time and effort to maintain the fix when it "costs" more than the problem does not compute. (For example, do you really think the U.S. Internal Revenue System [IRS] collects enough money from chasing down and fining tax evaders to pay for its operation?)

Refrain from adding complexity or maintenance overhead without a strong justification or easily quantifiable returns.

Pragmatic

Understanding optimal rates leads to real-world, or *pragmatic*, rates. Machines may initially run at an optimal rate, but inefficiencies creep in as time passes and diminish the rate very unnoticeably. This reality also affects applications and infrastructure: bloated code, a less selective SQL where clause, an extra network hop, server security scans, and dozens if not hundreds of other opportunities allow performance to dwindle from optimal to acceptable to customer-irritating.

The other side of the coin is the bad start that needs to be brought up to optimal before falling off slowly over time. I was helping a client with a performance problem after an 8TB Oracle database was replatformed. Prior to the replatforming, I had often helped the client tune the database, which had been running at a very acceptable pace. Oracle support was also involved in the triage. I have forgotten exactly what the Oracle engineer found that headed us toward resolution, but the bottom line was that new servers had a new Oracle software install that included minimal database configuration information. The configuration file (`spfile/init`) had been updated to show the correct database name, and other parameters to coincide with the existing database. What was missed were all the tuning-related parameters that had been adjusted to maintain performance. After an outage or two, the parameter settings from the configuration file still on the old database server were implemented, restoring performance to expectations.

Proximity Matters

Strict data movement design principles affect infrastructure strategy. Large data sets that travel long distances degrade performance, causing customer frustration. DBAs, developers, and DevOps teams have learned that applications running on application servers in close proximity to the source database outperform applications with greater distance between the database and application servers. Once the data volume is decreased—when a large data set is reduced to the minimally needed data for presentation to the customer—distance matters less. Proximity does matter; keeping that in mind serves the organization well.

A discussion that starts with the primary areas that DBAs control or have a high degree of influence upon (the database, OS, storage system, and application code) seems reasonable at this juncture.

Direct DBA Impact

DBAs are usually well versed in technologies that are tightly knitted to the database. For instance, a DBA may have more experience with UNIX kernel changes than a SA who has little experience managing database host systems. DBAs also find themselves defending the database because many people who report application problems like to call out database failures or slowness without evidence. After ensuring that the database is operating properly, DBAs, particularly those on DevOps teams, should continue to help troubleshoot the problem to make sure the database does not get a bad rap.

Database

Fast and reliable data delivery, combined with fast and secure data storage, obviously rank high on DBAs' top ten critical deliverables, whether internally hosted or externally hosted as a DBaaS solution. Specific controls pose a challenge. Internally hosted databases can be manipulated and tuned by using all available configuration parameters; DBaaS offerings include the ability to increase compute power, expand memory, and grow storage while enforcing restrictions that increase maintenance efforts and/or introduce risk that could impact other hosted customers. The level of configuration and tuning might vary, but expecting total control leads to disillusionment.

One of the most painstaking and often difficult problems to isolate and resolve is transaction locking. As data is changed, there is the chance that another process needs that data but cannot be granted access until the process that changed the data performs a commit. There can be several reasons for the delay between the data change and the transaction commit: the application code might have overlooked the need to commit before performing the next actions or the commit itself could be slow due to a foreign key constraint check in which the index is missing on the key column.

Locking can cause what appears to be a slowness issue; in reality, however, transactions that need the data have stopped processing. As the number of processes that need the data stack up, it becomes increasingly difficult to pinpoint the lock-holding process. As teams work through the problem by fixing code or implementing indexes on foreign keys, problem reports and other performance impacts should decrease, providing another opportunity to share the positive impact with leaders.

Operating System

Database performance and stability depend mightily on the underlying OS configuration and tuning. As mentioned earlier, out-of-the-box installs seem to fit smaller capacity loads. Scaling up the OS to support an e-commerce database load necessitates forethought and experience. DBAs reaching out to the cloud realize that scale can be addressed with virtual hosts and can use the opportunity to distribute load and manage capacity globally.

OS tuning in the cloud depends on the offering. IaaS solutions grant agility in OS building because you control the virtual OS and hosted applications or databases. PaaS solutions offer prebuilt OS flavors on which DBAs construct databases. DBaaS presents predefined database configurations for selection, which makes maintaining abstraction from the application necessary.

DBAs who consider these solutions to drive end-user experience improvements can moreover strengthen application resiliency and load distribution. Alternative database solutions, whether relational, flat file, network, indexed, key-value, or blockchain all require diligent analysis and piloting. Being able to construct and deconstruct virtually hosted databases brings about improved decisions based on data-backed results. Organizational inefficiencies that result in server builds taking weeks are impairments to progress.

DevOps team members should be able to interrogate the OS processing to determine what may be contributing to slowness. Tracing a sessions process reveals read and write calls, but can also identify latency caused by a shortage of semaphores. A lot can be learned by tracing process IDs, a learning task that can be done before a situation requires interrogation in real-time.

For best performance, the Oracle System Global Area (SGA) should consume a single memory segment. Using the interprocess communication facility command 'ipcs' with different flags details memory allocations, message queues, semaphores, and more.

Make sure you and the SA coordinate all changes to the database host.

Storage System

Highly redundant storage is now the expectation rather than an upgrade choice. Enterprise data not only performs within a transactional context but also drives customer–driven business decisions. Understanding customer behavior well enough to adjust product offerings, cross-sell, or offer "bolt-on" products for additional sales comes from data analytics.

DBAs act as guardians of the data to ensure availability and security. Data encryption is necessary not only to meet various governance requirements (PCI-DSS, HIPAA, Sarbanes-Oxley) but also to guard the company's reputation against data breaches and theft.

Storage systems with hardware encryption supply exceptional performance with little overhead. Leveraging proven vendor solutions takes storage off the table as a major concern because even basic storage arrays fit database read and write demands. High-end vendor solutions with multipathed, switched, fiber-connected solid-state drives (SSDs) or cache fronted mechanical drives offer read times that fit enterprise database prerequisites. Specialized databases that support financial exchanges or telecommunications move data into memory for nanosecond response times, subjugating storage to recording changes that are then immediately updated to memory for near-instantaneous access.

Measuring and communicating storage system value can be as simple as tracking a 30% response time reduction after increasing memory or adding an index and then sharing that information up the food chain. Contradictorily, millisecond improvements are harder for people to understand. "Oh wow, you decreased physical read time by a *whole* millisecond; aren't you special." Demonstrating that win demands context: I billion reads multiplied by I millisecond equals I million seconds or 16,666.66 minutes of reduced read time. Reducing read time from 6 milliseconds to 4 milliseconds is a 33% percent decrease. Framing milliseconds saved as a decrease percentage helps tell the story. Faster reads translate into more reads per time interval, which is an inverse correlation between the two measures (see Figure 7-4).

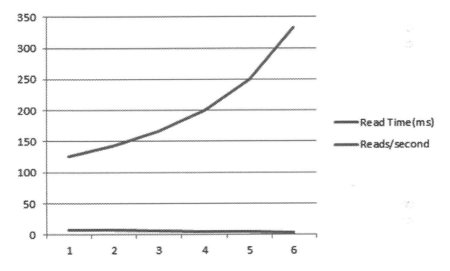

Figure 7-4. Read time reduction increases reads per second

Transaction durations decline and customer experience improves, benefiting from the load shift. Reports, analytics, and batch job run times should also shrink noticeably.

Although a millisecond is an eye blink for humans, it is a significant processing window for a computer

Application Code

Programmers work toward the primary objective of meeting the required data result that matches the business requirement. Performance and efficiency may not be considered initially—unless it is a DevOps team, of course. DBAs who spend time advocating for more selective query predicates and strategic data use can transform developer behavior toward mitigating performance degradation and other less-optimal practices.

Result Set

Too often, the data volume returned from a database query exceeds what is needed or should be managed. An application populating a pull-down window holding 5 selections has no need to return 1,000 rows from the database. Maintaining reasonable result sets minimizes compute, memory, storage, and network bandwidth waste.

Minimal Data Touch

Unnecessary data access wastes resources. A query selecting 1 million rows or documents when 10 are needed generates overhead detrimental to performance, not only for the calling query but also for all other work occurring in the database. DBAs can help developers construct code that reduces data access, thus improving performance. Where possible, imposing limitations on CPU and memory consumption by process or account can protect against runaway or inefficient code. Preventing "abuse" improves resiliency by mitigating system-wide impacts. Drawing on experience, DBAs can calibrate database and session controls to smooth database load and to thwart harmful resource spikes. NASCAR drivers are not constantly stomping the gas pedal and crushing the brake pedal to win races; instead, drivers maintain velocity and momentum at the highest speed possible to generate smooth, consistently fast laps. DBAs skilled in load management delve into operational processes to optimize resource consumption, dealing the same winning hand.

Code Reuse

Database optimizers make use of already loaded execution plans for matching statements to improve execution times and minimize cached SQL. Oracle creates a hash value for each SQL statement. It checks for that exact hash value in the library cache (LC). If the hash exists in the LC, Oracle uses the stored execution plan to execute the SQL. If the hash does not exist in the LC, the optimizer considers multiple execution plans by using different indexes, joins, and more to come up with the "best" plan, which takes time. This overhead measures in nanoseconds or very low milliseconds, a drop of water in the ocean of execution time. The multiplication factor for producing the hash and execution plan unnecessarily consumes CPU.

For example, consider these statements, hash values, and timings as a sequence of events:

Library cache (LC) empty.

1. `select EMP_name from emp;` hash 13579 1ms added to LC

2. `select EMP_name from emp;` hash 24680 1ms added to LC

3. `select EMP_name from emp;` hash 13579 70ns found in LC

The third SQL statement exactly matches statement 1, so the library LC already has the execution plan, and the time is reduced to 70 nanoseconds.

When it makes sense, using syntax-equivalent statements repeatedly means less database engine work (staying with the Oracle example). Oracle has bind variables that stand in for the actual value to maintain the same hash value, making it highly likely to find the execution plan in the LC. No matter the database vendor or technology, when SQL statements are understood, DBAs, developers, and DevOps engineers can reduce system load and improve response times.

Peripheral DBA Influence

Trusted and involved DBAs get invited to more nondatabase discussions 1) to make sure decisions and technologies do not harm the database environment; 2) as technical pros capable of assessing technologies and platforms; and 3) to influence others. DBAs may not be able to make the adjustments, but they can surely influence decisions and direction.

DBAs bridge the divide between development, infrastructure, and operations better than most IT roles. Knowing how to trace and improve code; being capable of defining infrastructure; and understanding load management, performance tuning, security, and recoverability formulate a technical resource that is capable of adding tremendous value to most strategic and tactical decisions. That value has been overlooked by DevOps until now.

Network

DBAs who are satisfied that the database is up and running without giving thought to the customer experience or end-to-end transactional performance may struggle integrating with a DevOps team. Being a DevOps team member means that DBAs accept responsibility for all aspects of product delivery, making singularly focused DBAs a hindrance to DevOps teams. Expanding contribution to solve system-wide problems, a DBA injects another perspective and set of experiences on which the team can capitalize.

Network influence on data delivery tops the charts of latency introducers. Each hop represents additional latency, continuously building as distance expands. Using the techniques described in Chapter 6, DBAs can dig deeply to mine the gold nuggets of improved performance. Partnering and building rapport with network engineers to collaborate in solving stability or performance challenges provides another channel to communicate wins.

End-User Devices

The type and suitability of end-user devices swings high to "gamer" PCs, smartwatches, and other Internet of Things (IoT) devices, making design decisions lean toward executing processes at the seat of power (i.e., processing power). Expecting to create an excellent customer experience with code executing on less-CPU-capable end devices does not make sense. Limiting data management and processing on the end-user device cuts to the bone, leaving only presentation concerns.

If end-user devices need to manage data infeed and code processing, keep expectations low by striving to keep processing close to the back end. As mentioned previously, tuning network packet size usually creates a maintenance headache with little return, so use it sparingly.

Abstracting the presentation layer from the code makes it easier to deliver information to end points. Having to create and maintain code for a multitude of device OSs and platforms becomes increasingly cost prohibitive as the number of versions increase.

Capacity

Beyond the operational aspects of database management, DBAs provide input concerning database growth based on business estimates. Although initial scope may be limited to storage and compute adjustments, DBAs must insist that other capacity considerations be assessed.

As storage increases, backups take longer and consume more storage media. If the database is being replicated to another site, the data volume increase consumes more replication circuit bandwidth and end-point storage.

An increase in users and or sessions may need to be offset with additional server memory and CPU to maintain acceptable or SLA–defined response times. Internal customers may be connected via terminal services that may respond more slowly under additional load, causing people to assume database slowness. DBAs who proactively address capacity holistically might save themselves from future headaches.

Recoverability

Database growth combined with increased user count means frequent recoverability reassessments. The database may now support an application considered critical, requiring a different recovery time objective (RTO). Reducing the application RTO means that the database recovery strategy may need to change. Asking "How should the database be backed up?" is the wrong question. Instead, ask this: "My database recovery requirement is *N* hours/days; how can that be done?" Recovery requirements drive backup solutions.

A database that previously backed up to tape in 8 hours may need to be backed up to virtual tape (disk) or disk storage that takes 1 hour, which means that the recovery time has been reduced from a minimum of 8 hours to about 1 hour. An application RTO of 24 hours does not mean that DBAs have 24 hours to recover the database. The database recovery must complete with enough time remaining for the application, services, and checkouts to occur before allowing full access for business operations.

A recovery point objective (RPO) sets expectations for acceptable data loss. For example, the business may request data loss to be less than 4 hours: RPO < 4 hours. DBAs can shrink the data loss with proper transaction logging and archiving.

DRaaS

Disaster Recovery as a Service (DRaaS) is an infant in the "as a service" world. It promises to reduce costs and complexity, so it will be exciting to watch this technology mature. Imagine not having to purchase and maintain duplicate data centers and equipment. DevOps teams need to track the growth and opportunity trajectories of this service.

Bringing It All Together

Plenty of value-adding opportunities exist, according to DevOps DBAs who have had opportunities to contribute beyond the general care and feeding of the database. Striving relentlessly to iteratively refine the application ecosystem while implementing database enhancements creates documentable case studies and fantastic "war story" material to share with leaders, team members, and peers.

Being able to communicate effectively to CIOs, CFOs, and other chiefs involves discerning which buttons to push for each. CFOs like to hear about cost decreases or revenue generation, but they could also be sponsoring a process improvement initiative to push new software features to customers more quickly. In that case, work done to reduce cycle time, incorporate database changes into the Agile pipeline, or remove wasted steps from the process gives the CFO great story material to share with customers.

Summary

Each of the touchpoints mentioned in this chapter generates detailed statistics that can be captured before and after problem events, changes, or proactive tuning of the database and supporting infrastructure. Massage the data for easy reading and clear communication of the facts to prove the team's worth.

DBAs who actively broaden their technical skill sets eventually and effectively transform the application and infrastructure landscape, within the context of DevOps, to improve performance, slim down processes, and improve customer experience.

Do not just solve technical problems or make technology work better; translate technical outcomes that can be advertised as solutions to business challenges that improved the organization and/or positively impacted people.

Automation and Code Control

DevOps is drawing a line in the sand: it is taking a stand for software product delivery excellence. As agile teams produce less-defective code more quickly, DevOps teams need to solidify the infrastructure foundation supporting the application. Both pieces are required to deliver software superbly and (more importantly) gain customer confidence in an organization's capability to operate well.

Customers and internal business teams demand and deserve applications that are available, reliable, fast, secure, and functionally precise, but also delivered nearly on demand. For decades, too many opportunities were missed or delayed because IT delivered software more slowly than the business need required. DevOps, along with Agile, refactors the software delivery process specifically to deliver faster, more accurately, and more highly resilient.

Company leaders need to see that technology investments are doing things to benefit the company. Revenue growth, a new sales channel, and reduced "lights-on" data center costs represent the tip of the iceberg of which the technology organization can gauge success. Automation accelerates product delivery, and code control reduces change coordination chaos while providing a recovery path.

© Michael S. Cuppett 2016
M. S. Cuppett, *DevOps, DBAs, and DBaaS*, DOI 10.1007/978-1-4842-2208-9_8

Craftsmanship

IT teams, whether marching as DevOps, plan, build, run, or technology-divided soldiers, understand that the mission of delivering software requires more than brute force implementations; instead, it is what one CIO calls it: "craftsmanship." The product quality difference between a metal works craftsman, or "Meister," and me wielding a 4-pound hammer and a few wrought iron bars does not require a rocket scientist to see. Yet "acceptable" has been the software building bar height for too long (decades) across the industry. Setting the bar much higher to rate software as "excellent" challenges project, development, testing, validation, and implementation methods, and also people's tried-and-true abilities.

As the culture and organization shift gears and accelerate, the goal is to complete software delivery without losing control and crashing head-on into a wall. Two mechanisms contributing directly to software delivery excellence are automation and code control. Ironically, they have existed for decades, yet are now being releveraged to push a change within companies and across the IT industry.

Human versus Computer

The human element introduces much of the imbalance (risk) that wreaks havoc on software delivery, especially when code release frequency slams into operational control. Two human perspectives—developers delivering code and operations teams protecting the ecosystem—tend to ignite all-night firefighting.

As mentioned in an earlier chapter, computers were first used to automate repetitive and mundane tasks, yet today many steps in the code build, test, release, deploy, operate, and support value stream are completed manually. DBAs may script a set of commands to keep from having to be command-line commandos during the release, but the overall process is very choppy and inefficient. And that DBA script is not likely to be in the source code repository.

Computers can repeat tasks repetitively and without errors far faster than humans, so it is surprising how often humans choose to repeat tasks. Changes moving from development to production include intermediate environments, sometimes requiring the change to be executed a handful or more times. Each manual change introduces the risk of a mistake, especially when the time elapsed since the last change is long enough to make recall fuzzy. Whether a step is overlooked or a few steps are completed in a different order, the environment may be different, and for sure the release process changed. Automating and validating the process removes the risk and improves execution time.

Getting Lean

DevOps, which derives many of its principles from lean manufacturing quality programs, rests a chunk of its success on eliminating waste (any task that does not create value) and shrinking cycle time. Figure 8-1 provides an example in which waste—extensive design, elaborate project management, and hardware acquisition on the front end and long documentation creation and release management on the back end—do not add enough value to the actual software development process, measured as cycle time, to justify the added time and cost.

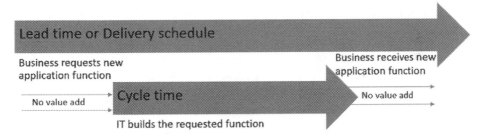

Figure 8-1. *Example of no value-add work surrounding the development cycle*

In contrast, DevOps shrinks the no value-add work to bare bones by having capacity in place to spin up virtual servers quickly, accepting the agile idea of frequent small releases that require much less release and operational readiness, and choosing to produce working software over documentation. Figure 8-2 reveals the leaner model.

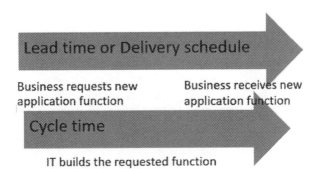

Figure 8-2. *Example of a lean delivery schedule in which the actual work, cycle time, accounts for most of the time*

As agile development practices continue to expand globally throughout the industry, Operations potentially becomes the bottleneck, which is never a good reputation characteristic. Rising DevOps acceptance and maturation affords a systemic approach to operational efficiency and process leaning, making Operations a facilitator of fantastic software delivery. Iterative improvements of operational processes bring the same value model as iterative software releases.

Conflicting Interests

Developers want to get new products, enhancements, and bug fixes through the pipeline quickly because they are incentivized to complete projects on time, budget, and schedule. Operations, including DBAs, want to preserve control, if for no other reason than not wanting to be on the phone overnight or all weekend, explaining why the company's most critical application is metaphorically a smoking heap of elephant dung. Control—change control or change management—provides the perception of stabilization or risk reduction while deceiving us all because most of us have experienced the opposite effect. Even with extra prerelease diligence performed, large releases still rattle business operations when the code "rubber" meets the production "road."

DBAs embracing DevOps have the occasion and obligation to offer better and faster ways to make and process database changes. When the SDLC road trip has to divert onto an old country road to pick up schema changes, only to backtrack down that same old country road, inefficiency (read that as time lost) breeds. DevOps tools facilitate schema change automation that can be inducted into the automated change management process. Being confident in the automated build process allows DBAs to deliver consistent deployments while staying aligned with the progressing code necessitating the database change.

Automation Benefits

Benefits stack up quickly with automation incorporation: shortening the software release cycle, reducing defects, integration evidence, exhaustive testing, repeatability, auditability, performance scrutiny, and documented results. DevOps DBAs produce value and reduce effort through automation.

I remember one Oracle shop in which a DBA would manually check all the production databases every day. The process took 4 to 5 hours every workday. A new DBA joined the team, and, as the newbie, was given the honor of taking over the daily checks. Day 1: the newbie watched the DBA most recently charged with performing the check complete the checks. Day 2: manually completed the checks with oversight from the other DBA. Day 3: manually performed the checks and built scripts to automate the checks. Day 4: ran the scripts and double-checked the results manually. Once verified, the

DBA scheduled the checks to execute the next morning, with the outcomes e-mailed to the DBA team and director. Day 5: the DBA read the e-mail and was recognized by the director for being "innovative." That sounds like a great first week!

Release Cycle Shrink

Retail *shrink* usually means that employees and/or customers are stealing from a store. This kind of shrink is bad. Reducing the period of time needed to code, promote, test, and validate included infrastructure and application changes that are needed to ready the next release by "stealing" back time—time available but not leveraged—helps shrink the duration needed for each release. There are at least three "times" that need to be refactored.

Testing

Do not do it . . . manually. Developers produce abundant amounts of usable (bug-free) code if they are allowed to focus. Unfortunately, developer efficiency degrades when testing, documentation, project scheduling, and meetings divert time and energy. DBAs incur these same distractors, plus they spend time doing operational support. The easiest distraction to gain back time for punching code comes from minimizing manual testing. DBAs have the same opportunity to achieve maximum output over time. DBAs who assert themselves as DevOps team members need to start thinking like developers for database changes.

You should understand that Agile development practices include guidelines to reduce meeting duration while increasing communication. Agile frameworks Scrum, Kanban, and XP (Extreme Programming) focus developer effort on producing code. The Agile Manifesto (http://agilemanifesto.org) includes "Working software over comprehensive documentation"[1] as a value statement. Further, the manifesto states one of its 12 principles as "Working software is the primary measure of progress."[2]

Testing beyond compile and simple function execution belongs in the automation realm. Leveraging virtualization automation enables DBAs to recur testing until an acceptable product persists. Spinning up a database server from an infrastructure as code template, replicating the current production footprint to which proposed database schema changes, performing tuning tweaks, or applying and testing access privilege grants are doing DevOps. First-time execution may reveal object invalidations triggered by the schema change due

---

[1]http://agilemanifesto.org
[2]http://agilemanifesto.org/principles.html

to dependency references. Changing a table column referenced by an index that uses that table column may cause the index to be invalidated. The index fix has to be incorporated into the schema change code. Testing the database changes until perfecting implementation eases staff deployment tensions and mitigates change-related errors. Although this cycle seems tedious, tools make the process easier. Anything and everything that can be automated to excessively test builds, changes, code, configurations, or anything testable is a win for product delivery.

As changes are checked into the repository, the CI server is ready to pounce. The CI server may react on every change commit or be configured to run at a scheduled time (the industry suggests at least once daily). Check-in occurs after developers build code and run simple functional testing to prove that the expected results did happen. The CI server has responsibility for ensuring that the objects representing the delta between the previous run and the new run are tested and proved to work as designed in the context of the whole application in the planned infrastructure environment. Once the code branches pass all testing, a new product version is created as the code trunk. User acceptance testing, or product owner assessment, still plays a valuable role in the SDLC. Here is one aspect for which iterative development helps to ensure product success. The user interface (UI) significantly defines the user experience (UX). You may make the best curry chicken on the planet, but your now unhappy customer will not try it if it is served in a plastic bucket. Poor presentation has plagued software development: your customer may decide to not use the application, or efficiency suffers if an employee must use the company's application to fulfill job requirements. Overcoming this typically late stage mess means gathering immediate feedback from the customer or product owner early in the development process.

Iterative development includes producing an early model or prototype of the UI. Although there might not be a single line of code behind the storefront, the product owner still sees the interface and has the opportunity to recommend moving forward, make a few adjustments, or give the team the opportunity for a "do over." No matter the outcome, timely feedback at this point does not result in expensive rework.

Scrum uses *sprints*, predetermined time allocations, to manage work demand. Daily sprints are designed for developers to select a unit of work that can be completed that day, making iteration a good fit. The team's day 2 UI presentation has the benefit of the product owner's feedback from the previous day, which improves the UI to better imitate the requested look and feel. Henceforth, daily refinements and cosmetic enhancements further improve the UI. Scrum also uses sprints to define the duration for when production-ready software can be deployed (2 weeks is a common interval). As the 2-week sprint ends, the UI is fully developed and fully vetted.

Parallelism

Getting work done without actually doing the work is awesome. Granted, you had to do something smart upfront, with repeatability as the goal. Testing was a step traditionally performed by a QA team after the software development completed. Two distinct phases, coding and testing, extended the release cycle. Agile and DevOps are adamant that automated testing should occur early in the code process. Many recommend that unit tests be created before the code unit is written, making the programming goal meeting the expected test results. Once the unit is written and checked in to the source code repository, the CI process begins testing the code: testing the code integrated with the rest of the programs, including checking for performance and security gaps. This process allows people to do other work in parallel. No, QA testers are not out of a job; instead, they focus on ensuring that defects are discovered by creating extensive, deep-diving test code to hunt down software flaws. The act of testing is automated, and the test creation can be supplemented by redirected QA team members.

As DBA changes are injected into the workflow as just more code, testing needs to broaden in scope to include the database code. DBAs and QA team members should follow the same advice as often as feasible: build the test and then the code. Interrogating database schema changes may include verifying the metadata definition. Inserting or updating data in that modified column seems to be a reasonable test. Again, test for invalidations caused by a change to append the corrective action to the deployment script. This could be the process flow:

1. Capture current settings

2. Make changes

3. Verify changes

4. Check for invalidations

5. Fix invalidations

6. Record changes for audit

7. Recheck for invalidations

Whether the fix is a call to another script or a dynamic SQL statement build matters not. The critical element is not leaving a broken object in place.

As people work in parallel while testing, the testing itself should also execute in parallel. Crunching the CI cycle into the tiniest possible time slot positions testing in several ways: if a problem occurs, retesting can be completed without interfering with post-testing efforts or running into the business day; testing can be repeated to validate results; and additional testing can be performed without extending the test window, so additional test cycles can occur.

Moving from once daily to twice daily testing is not possible if testing take 15 hours running serially. Many threads that run in parallel may complete the testing in 4 hours, so testing can occur twice or even four times per day.

Not Working Does Not Mean Not Working

Just because you have finished working for the day—after checking in your code to let the CI servers start chugging through automated testing—the work has not finished. So making something happen during your "down" window seems like a smart way to prepare for the next day while you complete other tasks.

Time and money are the finite resources that prevent IT shops from maintaining the perfect infrastructure and delivering every value-add business request. Managing to best outcome, effective IT leaders set priorities by giving staff the flexibility and tools to produce the best product. That practice has become easier as DevOps and its associated tool products have matured. DevOps team members know that product delivery cycles must contract; DBAs have to be able to meet the same timelines. Being able to get work done while not actually working benefits all.

Identifying distinct units of work that can be completed automatically and without human overwatch is not new. IT pros have for years executed backups, index builds or rebuilds, ETL processes, data scrubs, and other work during off-hours. DevOps expands the type of work that can be included. For instance, a DBA may spend the day perfecting (or at least attempting to perfect) a database-provisioning process. To validate, the DBA may construct a series of test builds scheduled to run overnight. Although the DBA is relaxing, maybe writing a book, testing hacks, or building a gaming computer, the work gets done, builds an audit log, and awaits review the next morning. Repeating this cycle for a few days should be enough time to consider the build process viable.

Not leveraging nonwork hours would be wrong, just plain wrong. DBAs tend to never be wrong; just ask one of us! (Just a joke, my developer friends.)

Automating Out Errors

DBAs who repeatedly execute command sequences or scripts contribute to error origin, bottlenecks, and inefficiency. Agile development accelerates the software build process, leading to rapid code deployment readiness with proven error reduction. If the monthly production rollout involves 15 minutes of code errorless deployment and 6 hours of error-prone database work, DBAs surely realize that the database deployment process expounds what "being out of kilter" means. Inconsistency results in problems; automation instills consistency. Even if the automation produces the wrong outcome, it returns a consistently incorrect outcome, which can be easily isolated and rectified.

DevOps mandates extensive testing for each element within the value proposition of better software faster. Thoroughly testing each foundational application component (program function, procedure, API, microservice, container, database call, or audit service) represents the starting point for error elimination because an error is never allowed to progress. DevOps teams should continuously assert the mantra "never progress errors." As the code advances from singular functional purpose to an integrated form, intense testing must examine every attainable execution derivative to ensure code compatibility and expected outcomes, without error. As code travels from the branch to the trunk, automated regression testing provides the final vetting of the software before it is considered release- or deployment ready, again 100% error free. Taking advantage of every minute of the day to perform work without your participation increases your overall effectiveness and contribution to the organization.

Zero Defects!

DevOps shifts the "defects can be worked around" cultural acceptance to "no bug lives past today" diligence. "Today" sounds aggressive, albeit improbable in infantile DevOps shops; however, team members begin to value quality out of respect for the customer, leading to the latter mantra. As DevOps matures in the organization, the improbable becomes routine. By not having to plan according to a monthly release schedule, DBAs have the flexibility and empowerment to correct defects quickly if the need arises. Remember that excessive testing spawns flawless releases. Maintaining zero defects across the IT supply chain challenges existing infrastructure and deployment paradigms, making DevOps the release hero. The effort spent on prerelease testing provides a better return than the effort spent troubleshooting and determining root cause and plausible remediation of the production system.

Broadening the concept to include the infrastructure as code is not limited to server or database provisioning. The right devices combined with the right tools means that load balancers can be automatically updated during rolling releases. Moving away from sequential team efforts (team A completes task 1, team B completes task 2, team A completes task 3, and so forth) decimates error opportunity through excessive automation that is not used until it runs correctly and efficiently, leaving behind a comprehensive audit trail. Not introducing errors from manual sequential change steps is a great step toward maintaining a zero-defect posture.

Death by Workaround

Workarounds have a nasty habit of sticking around longer than expected, and for sure until there is a chance to cause further disruption or grief. Imagine "softening" application access to deliver a large-revenue customer's demanded application enhancement. Great, the customer is happy, so that gets registered as a win for the team. Six months later, your company is being sued by the same customer who blames your squishy access security for a major data breach. Internal workarounds create similar problems, mainly because the production workaround never gets applied to the preproduction or development environments. New features rolling toward production then pass all testing but fail when released. After hours of multiteam investigations, the forgotten workaround is rediscovered as the culprit.

Platform consistency must include workarounds introduced into production. DBAs implementing workarounds must incorporate the workaround into the build automation to ensure consistency in the nonprod environments to eliminate production surprises. This obligation includes positive workarounds, such as adding an index to improve query performance. Adding an index seems innocuous until another query that performed well in development and testing runs ten times more slowly in production. The availability of the workaround index caused the optimizer to select an execution plan that was not previously obtainable.

Two equally important mandates—to drive out defects before the production release and, when a production defect is discovered, to redirect energy toward its elimination—amp up software quality so that customers notice, providing you with a competitive edge through customer loyalty.

Orchestration

Evolving from automation to orchestration includes threading together individual automations to build an efficient workflow. After meticulously building, testing, and validating various automation packages used to construct web, app, and database servers; test data loads; and finally verification scripts, stepping through a logical process makes sense. Although each automation can be executed in isolation, the true power of automation comes from purposefully designed workflows that meet expected build demand. A developer needing a new application environment would appreciate and benefit from a stringed set of automations. An easy click or two starts a cascading progression of web, app, and database server builds; test data loading; and validation. This list is simplistic, but the positive results are nearly unlimited. Orchestration is illustrated by security patching and scanning; code compilation; firewall and load balancer configurations; monitoring agent installs; synthetic transactions; auditing log transmission; backup configuration; encryption; certificates, metadata loads; and everything else that needs to be built, configured, or reported combining to provide the needed infrastructure and application, which enables further code development or production deployment.

Orchestration offers amiable outcomes. DevOps engineers produce automation designed to allow the consumer—DBA or developer—to customize changes, whether allowing the selection of different database products or digesting a spreadsheet of access requests. Pieces from here, there, and over there align to produce an expected product. KISS (keep it simple, stupid) brutally challenges us to not do what we tend to do too often: overengineer. To summarize Einstein, "If you can't explain it simply, you do not understand it." The general challenge for IT team members is to not overcomplicate things from a lack of understanding. Simple, elegant, and effective solutions take much more brilliance to implement. Making it possible for DevOps team members to hit the "easy" button to produce needed environments requires significant behind-the-scenes orchestration, during which design and performance are critical, complexity is unwelcomed, and the results are astonishing.

Automated testing provides a means to complete 99% of the testing needed before product launch, leaving the final most critical 1% to be done manually: user acceptance testing or (for Agile) product owner acceptance. Sitting down with the customer, walking through the product to determine usability, cosmetics, workflow, understandability, and general awesomeness can be a disillusioning experience. Many application products have died on release after millions of dollars were invested because the product was unusable for the customer. Iterative building, revealing, product owner feedback, and realignment using agile practices intends to stop product DOA scenarios. Although having frequent face time with the product owner to demonstrate the product and accept feedback favors final product acceptance, surprises can happen, so user acceptance is a critical path approval. Because of the recurrent product display and owner feedback, user acceptance may take 15 minutes, whereas a waterfall user acceptance test could take days or even weeks (remember that waterfall projects are relatively larger in scope per release).

Great testing requires an aggressive posture: DevOps team members openly challenge each other, including those who say, "My tests will crush your code!" Keeping score can add to the friendly competiveness.

Performance

Although developers and DBAs never sit down to discuss how to introduce slowness into an application environment, not proactively working to ensure that performance meets expectations does not sound much different. Purposefully setting performance expectations for code execution seems like a responsible act.

Modified code should execute at least as fast as the previous version, given that no functional elements have been added. Based on how other code performs, extrapolating base performance expectations is possible. For instance, if most production searches, regardless of the search criteria, complete in .1 second on average, you can state that all search code must execute and return the result set in .1 second or less. As you mature the performance standards, searches may get divided into search groupings: simple versus complex or structured data versus unstructured data. As experience grows among the team, and analytics provide undisputable evidence for performance, metrics selection that include data inserts, updates, and deletes also needs to have defined performance expectations. It astonishes me how many times I have heard, "The update took only half a second." I like to remind that person that half a second is "like forever" in computer time. DevOps has also brought about the mindset that not only does code (application or database) have to produce the correct outcome; it also has to produce it without negatively impacting performance.

Code Control

Gaining control over DBA code first requires the code to be managed like the application code, by using a source code repository. Versioning, check-in, and check-out provide an audit trail, making it much easier to determine when an error was introduced, or perhaps a change proceeded or did not get applied with the matching code change. The CI test executions should catch these problems, allowing DBAs to adjust the code and resubmit. This additional accountability is good for DBAs. Whether implementing infrastructure as code for a database install or schema build, a data load for testing, or a simple create index script, all the code needs to be pulled by version from the source code repository for execution.

Check-in Snowballs

CI servers anxiously await source code check-ins because that is when CI servers get to shine. Remember that everything is considered code. As DBAs, developers and other team members commit changes to the source code repository, the CI server goes to work by testing each autonomous code element. If hundreds of people commit changes before the daily trunk integration, the CI server work snowballs quickly into a significant workload. Fortunately, the automated testing progresses proficiently through the test sequence leading to a deploy-ready state.

Continuous Delivery (CD)

DBAs participate in CD by uniting with DevOps team members to deliver the promise of always–ready database server deployment and database application code. Unlike developers who focus primarily on application delivery,

DBAs contribute to infrastructure database builds and application elements. DBA infrastructure as code assimilates with the OS build package to facilitate automated database server provisioning. Additionally, DBA schema, stored procedure, trigger, auditing, and data loading code aids application delivery.

Easy to Roll Back or Roll Over

By design, extensive CI testing should discover and report bugs. DBAs implicating code defects need to resolve them quickly because it is imperative that the application always be in a deployable state. DBAs can refer to the source code repository to determine whether the defective code should be rolled back to a known working version or to roll over the defective code with a newer version. Perhaps a needed schema change was overlooked, causing a mismatch between the database and the application code. A DBA could quickly build a new version containing the schema change, commit into the source code repository, and allow the CI server to execute the test sequence again, successfully this time. DevOps truly leans toward advancing code rather than rolling back to code that obviously needed to be replaced.

Auditable

Version control provides a very beneficial change: an audit trail. Auditing serves many purposes, whether providing responses to external governing bodies or internal security or audit team inquiries, the electronic paper trail tells the necessary story. For DevOps continuous delivery, the versioning supports the bug-free, application-readiness premise. Code failing the "shock-and-awe" quantity of functional and regression testing demands immediate remediation. Interrogating the code versions makes it easy to determine where the defect was introduced.

Managing Chaos

IT shops continue to struggle managing large and complex infrastructures. DBAs struggle with the database subset of infrastructure, not to mention the application demand on the databases. Scale introduces variability risk. A DBA team that manages a handful of databases may be able to manually maintain the databases, keeping deployments consistent, and maintaining performance and security while assuring recoverability. Amping up the number of databases to 1,000 with few staff additions makes the scale and scope unmanageable.

Drift management software helps keep basic infrastructure configuration inline, leaving change management to the DBAs. Determining the lowest common denominator pertaining to database configuration becomes the base build template to be applied for every build. Being confident that every deployed database has the same attributes allows DBAs to focus elsewhere. The next level may be scale, where a development deployment configuration includes less compute and memory consumption. For builds, having a size option prevents resource waste while still helping with overall environment control. Exceptions, aka special features, become the last frontier in which significant deployment variation can be introduced.

Minimizing database variation while empowering application and business capabilities can be balanced. Forward-thinking and well-planned builds shrink the scale risk by limiting the number of possible database gestations deployed. Variable consistency seems oxymoronic; no wonder so many companies have successfully leveraged it. Car makers have worked diligently to maintain parts consistency—working to use the same parts in as many models as possible while still being able to offer a variety of models to customers. Printer manufacturers separated power and language component from the core printer product, making printers consistent and offering variation by customer geography. A base printer, to which the needed power module and cord and language set is added, can be shipped anywhere in the world, making the printer function for the local environment. The cost savings and product maintenance savings have validated the variable consistency idea.

Bare Bones Disaster Recovery

Having an application data backup and the source code repository means that you can recover the environment, period. Infrastructure as code can be used to provision host servers—anywhere you can find the resources, deployment automation can configure the application, and the data recovery completes readiness for business operations. That is the power of Agile and DevOps pertaining to disaster recovery. Sure, that is an unlikely recovery strategy for many organizations, but having the capability reveals program maturity. After all, fully automated server provisioning, application code deployment, and data recovery are foundational DevOps goals. This capability can also be leveraged to disperse the application for geographical separation and multivendor cloud redundancy.

▓ **Note** For context, *disaster recovery* pertains to the catastrophic loss of a data center requiring production processing to be recovered at an alternate, geographically separated data center.

Disaster recovery can be done in many ways. Personally, I like the 5 Rs:

1. Replicate: disk replication for the most critical systems

2. Recover: secondary systems can be recovered from virtual tape backups

3. Redirect: DRaaS makes it possible to redirect connections to the secondary system

4. Rebuild: use infrastructure as code templates to spin up virtual hosts

5. Retire: it may make more sense to not invest in noncritical and/or antiquated systems recoveries

Tribal Knowledge Retained

Staff turnover happens, but when the source code repository contains all the database-related code, you are much less likely to hear the just-hired DBA say, "I have no idea how the previous DBA implemented that change." Being able to check the source code repository, change management logs, and deployment logs provides the details needed to understand how a change was implemented. The automation also allows code to continue progressing without having to wait for the new DBA to "get up to speed." Sure, the new DBA needs to quickly understand the database automation and be ready to modify the code as needed, but as DevOps preaches, no one person should be the only resource capable of doing a specific task. Other team members should be able to handle code modifications and even simple database changes if a DBA is not available. Speed and control are benefits driven by excellent code-progressing automation, not by more and more people talking about risk.

Summary

Application code, various configuration settings, database startup parameters, test scripts, and infrastructure as a code templates are but a few of the system elements managed in the source code repository. The CI server needs to be able to access versions required for testing, which leads to ready-to-deliver software.

Automation allows for more testing in less time, making it possible to execute an ever-expanding suite of tests to truly strip the code of defects. Designing scripts for testing, data loads, host and database builds, and app and web server builds facilitates on-demand host builds, allowing DevOps teams to test new coding techniques or server configurations without being penalized for taking risks. Failed attempts exist only until the host can be destroyed, soon to be replaced by another virtual host ready for more experimentations. Teams that are no longer bound by week- or month-long server build and database install processes are freed up to take time to optimize host and database configuration.

DBaaS, IaaS, and PaaS

Proper orientation, or level-setting ourselves, allows us to leverage the knowledge foundation we already have to gain additional knowledge. Software as a Service (SaaS) is an acknowledged winner in the "as a Service" product realm, so let's start there before engaging with our chapter title offerings.

SaaS

Software as a Service (SaaS) offerings have successfully penetrated organizations across industries, continuingly growing market share while embedding the term *as a Service* into our language:

> *...worldwide SaaS and cloud software performance by vendor in 2014 and anticipated performance through 2019. The cloud software market reached $48.8 billion in revenue in 2014, representing a 24.4% YoY growth rate. IDC expects cloud software will grow to surpass $112.8 billion by 2019 at a compound annual growth rate (CAGR) of 18.3%. SaaS delivery will significantly outpace traditional software product delivery, growing nearly five times faster than the traditional software market and becoming a significant growth driver to all functional software markets. By 2019, the cloud software model will account for $1 of every $4.59 spent on software."*[1]

---

[1]`https://www.idc.com/getdoc.jsp?containerId=257397`

© Michael S. Cuppett 2016
M. S. Cuppett, *DevOps, DBAs, and DBaaS*, DOI 10.1007/978-1-4842-2208-9_9

SaaS is simply the delivery of an application that is supported by infrastructure (and includes a database if needed) that is offered to individuals or companies that need the functionality of the application but do not want to develop, host, or support the environment. I very recently watched a television advertisement for Namely, a provider of human resources management software. An e-mail was in my inbox this week from FreshBooks, a small business accounting software provider. The big dogs such as Microsoft, Oracle, CA, salesforce, and more are still positioning for market dominance.

SaaS is the pinnacle of the "as a Service" offerings because the provider does the care and feeding of the solution. You need only to connect to the provider's site, log in, and then start doing business (after you make the agreed-upon payments, of course). SaaS offerings can scale to support large organizations while allowing small businesses to use the same application because costs are driven by consumption.

SaaS Ecosystem

SaaS combines the full infrastructure stack (physical hardware with compute and memory resources, network connectivity, attached storage, OSs, database, and a well-designed application) hosted in an industry best-in-class data center with exceptional redundancies for power, network ingress and egress, and environmental controls (see Figure 9-1).

The SaaS delivery model simplifies business and IT operations for companies. To leverage SaaS, organizations need to connect to the product portal, usually with a web browser, to begin using the application. In some cases, the com-

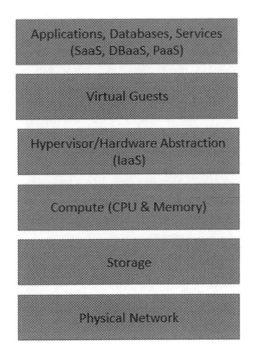

Figure 9-1. Example of a technology stack

pany may load an initial data set, possibly customer or product information. Smartphones, tablets, or workstations connected through an Internet service provider are easily attainable and manageable.

Businesses of all sizes can easily evolve from desktop, in-house, or commercial off the shelf (COTS) applications, in which software installation and occasional software upgrades are troublesome and backups are not done (or not done properly or frequently enough), to SaaS. Relieved from the IT administrative burden, organizations execute on strategic drivers to grow revenue and market share. SaaS adds value such that the customer's only concern becomes application availability, although confident the provider has the capability to keep the application available. SaaS offerings range from simple to complex applications, at least from the customer's functional capabilities perspective. E-mail provides limited capabilities compared with a customer relationship management (CRM) application. For the developers creating the products, the complexity may be similar: the customer perceives the products differently. People approach e-mail expectantly, but they may approach CRM apprehensively.

"as a Service"

Service offerings come in many flavors, each with an affinity toward specific customers who need particular capabilities. These offerings relieve IT departments from the drudgery and costs surrounding asset procurement, installation, maintenance, and ongoing support while delivering very functional, highly available, and well-performing environments. "as a Service" produces a strategic opportunity for organizations. For example, organizations are unlikely to invest in developing or operating a human resources, accounts payable, or procurement application if they are currently searching for a solution. Software development and hosting companies provide applications and infrastructure, allowing organizations to pay for these applications as a service.

Executable functions common to organizations are not where companies look for competitive advantages. Therefore, "as a Service" products are expeditious and frugal selections recognized for ease of use, competitive pricing, and corporate financial prudence. Predictable cash flow (knowing how much is being paid monthly as opposed to large, periodic capital outlays) combined with hands-off administration redirects staff focus and purpose to pursue strategic opportunities. IT can energize business growth, eliminate waste, manage the value stream, and deliver on customer expectations to create competitive advantages.

Because "as a Service" offerings are consumption based, pricing scales in correlation to business growth. For instance, if your company is growing and hiring more people, expect the human resources SaaS provider to increase fees based on an agreed–upon pricing scale.

"as a Service" opportunities break down complexity to simplify investment and operating decisions: which layers of the technology stack should or can others manage better than us? Let them do it. Or strategically, which layers of the stack must we manage for competitive advantage or data security? We should turn everything else over to a provider.

IaaS

Infrastructure as a Service (IaaS), also known as utility computing, includes the physical infrastructure: for example, CPU, memory, storage, network, and power. It also has an IaaS virtualization layer, also called a data center OS. Here, the customer consumes resources to execute and manage the rest of the stack.

Virtual host migrations between IaaS environments, on-premise to cloud, cloud to cloud, and cloud to on-premise are the same tasks across a variety of host configurations and locations. Physical server migrations are tougher but doable because you have to convert the physical server into a virtual server; if possible, I recommend virtualizing locally before migrating. Technically, IaaS migration work is not much different from the effort needed to move from an existing server to a new server; the primary difference is the distance between the source and target computers when using a provider's offering.

Figure 9-2 compares the purposes for IaaS, PaaS (discussed in the next section), and SaaS.

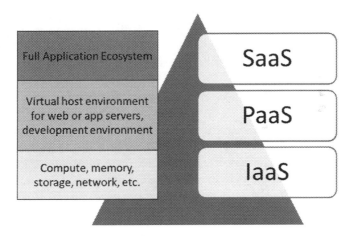

Figure 9-2. Purpose comparison between IaaS, PaaS, and SaaS

IaaS offerings provide the "shortest" stack, leaving customers with design flexibility. Google Cloud Platform, AWS, and Azure are a few IaaS offerings.

PaaS

Platform as a Service (PaaS) really appeals to the software development crowd. Focusing on building great software products without the distractions of building and operating infrastructure increases developer productivity and probably morale. By offering a variety of OSs, programming environments, containers, and middleware technologies, PaaS enables the software development company to provision environments and quickly start developing and testing products. Whether the company plans to make the software available for organizations to run internally or in the cloud, the software should be able to run on multiple OSs without specific configuration changes. Not wanting to build guests with OSs or middleware software, the company simply provisions the environment needed.

Businesses can also take advantage of the PaaS solution, whether for development or production, because the environment provides flexible configurations. One business I am familiar with has been porting web services to an on-premise PaaS environment, including containerization. The company is basically consolidating web services on disparate platforms written in several programming languages to the PaaS environment using a single programming language.

Off-premise PaaS means that the provider's automation performs the builds and makes the environment available to the customer. Relegating to customers the power to select the best platform based on their development strategy delivers value while allowing the consumer to serve a broader customer base without having to own every potential customer configuration on which the software may be deployed.

"Born on the web" companies (those that build applications in the cloud) can leverage PaaS. Imagine going to a PaaS provider site and provisioning a Windows Server environment with IIS, a SQL Server database guest, and another Windows server. You then add your preferred development tool onto it and let the developers have at it. A new app could be available for sale in days, if not sooner. Within a week, the company can generate revenue. Next app!

SaaS, IaaS, and PaaS fit a unique base customer requirement: SaaS meets application needs; PaaS meets development, web and app tier, services, and container deployment requirements; and IaaS allows full data center server compliment without having to invest in building a data center.

Although there are other interesting "as a Service" offerings such as Communications as a Service (CaaS), DBaaS needs to be our principal focus for the rest of the chapter.

DBaaS

DBaaS sits between PaaS and SaaS, at least in my eyes (see Figure 9-3).

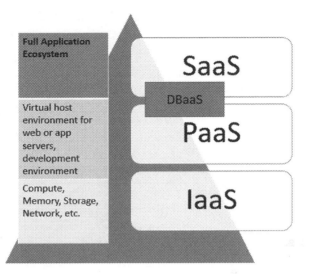

Figure 9-3. DBaaS fits between PaaS and SaaS

The crucial differences between them are that you pay for everything needed to use an application with SaaS (you configure nothing); PaaS solutions may be web or application servers, containers with microservices, or a combination; and DBaaS allows you to select which database you need and is more likely to be implemented as the only technology in the environment.

You won't be doing much beyond selecting the database product and a few sizing options because the provider's automation builds the environment and database based on a few selections you made concerning usage. As with SaaS, the DBaaS provider manages the technology; the customer provides the data. CRM SaaS offerings obviously include a database for data storage, but realize that the back end could be a DBaaS environment. It makes sense that a SaaS provider would use a DBaaS solution for the data.

For a DBA, fulfilling the demand for a data store needs to be a flexible, business-driven, and cost-conscious act. For example, using DBaaS to provide development and testing environments that can be spun up and then destroyed provides the necessary flexibility to keep a project moving without having to purchase additional servers or database licenses. Along that same line, the company may have an internal homogenous development infrastructure used to produce application software. To then certify the application against other databases, DBaaS facilitates the need at a reasonable price with technical simplicity.

DBaaS also allows DBAs to provide the best-fitting database for the job. The type of data to be stored, how the data is retrieved, and how often the data is modified or replaced drive the database selection.

DBaaS fits especially well when the company's data repositories are separated from the application, creating the amiability of using different databases as business requirements change.

If your business is data, you want to be able to manage it while making it available to customers. Customers paying to look at or retrieve your data need simple methods (APIs or services) for the access. Google provides data. Google stores and indexes data for people to access by using the search engine. DBAs understand that the volume and types of data make using a single vendor's product challenging, so having the flexibility to select different databases to fit specific needs leads to better solutions and (very likely) significant performance improvements.

Leveraging DBaaS for DevOps

DevOps requires speed and agility based on a foundation of lean practices and simplicity. New projects, whether for new functionality or improving existing code, no longer require DBAs to figure out how to fit new data requirements into existing relational databases. Although relational databases have served us well and continue to be excellent transaction recorders and systems of record, not every data requirement fits into the relational model. Unfortunately, DBAs have had to figure out how to make various-shaped data fit into the relational model, which is not necessarily the best performing or manageable situation. Companies that have made sizeable investments in database technologies may be reluctant to spend additional money on DBaaS; but not doing so may unfortunately limit competiveness, the flexibility needed to meet customers' demands, and application functionality and performance.

Architecture

The design processes for a database in the cloud (DBaaS) and for an on-premise cloud are very similar. Two aspects demand additional scrutiny: latency and configuration flexibility. Otherwise, architecture decisions for DBaaS are typical of what you have been doing for years, which makes the learning curve short.

Latency

Network packet travel time becomes a design challenge when the database is hosted in a location that is geographically distant from other components supporting the application. Even 20 milliseconds of ping time between an application server and a database server results in 40 milliseconds of latency for each network send and acknowledge pairing. Transactions involve many packets, so (doing basic math) we know that 100 packets would result in 4,000 milliseconds, or 4 seconds, of latency, not including the database processing time. Four seconds, in most instances, is already an unacceptable response time; customers may abandon your application to find an alternative. The 4-second example is a bit extreme, but it does demonstrate how quickly latency can impact business operations and customer experience.

Some protocols address latency better than others, such as acknowledging only every tenth packet. However, for design purposes, using the worst-case scenario (40 milliseconds per send and receive in this example) is recommended, primarily because it can be applied to every database product talking to every middleware product. If the implemented solution keeps latency under the design value, the better-than-expected application response time is a win for the design team.

Configuration Inflexibility

Experienced DBAs—not necessarily old DBAs—are used to being able to finely tune the database. They then work with the OS administrator to tune the kernel, optimizing I/O and storage throughput, and possibly even working with the network and client support teams to boost network and client performance by rightsizing the packet MTU and client buffer, which can also be a latency factor. With DBaaS, DBAs generally have limited ability to tune for performance. Available selections, some as simple as small, medium, and large, can be very limiting. If the environment is based on database product and size, careful planning is needed to prevent capacity problems too soon in the lifecycle. Fortunately, virtualized environments include the advantage of adding capacity with a few mouse clicks, but DBAs would still rather not have to explain why the business has to absorb unplanned costs so early in the product lifespan.

When it is considered, simplification is the saving aspect for configuration inflexibility. Although being able to fine tune a database may be needed, the effort becomes non-value-adding when it is really not necessary. If the application can run well using a very simple database implementation, consider that a good thing. For products that rely on extreme performance or synchronous writes, the inability to properly engineer the database implementation may be problematic; fortunately, that applies to a small percentage of databases running in our world.

Scalability

A database does not often shrink, and it could be stated that customers have never provided feedback saying the an application is too fast, or even that it would be acceptable for response times to be 1.5 seconds instead of 1 second.

So based on experience, DBAs know that performance must be maintained or improved to keep both the business and customers happy.

As mentioned earlier, DBaaS, or a virtualized database solution, includes the benefit of being able to scale solutions by adding CPU and memory resources on the fly. The preferred method is an automatic resource increase based on triggers. For instance, memory can be increased by *N*% if free memory falls below 5%. Or .25 virtual CPU can be added when CPU usage exceeds 98% for more than 5 minutes. Consider also the decision to be on a shared environment, in which growth applies to each entity hosted, compared with selecting a dedicated implementation. The latter comes at premium costs, but provides segregation.

Recoverability

Three primary risks need to have mitigation plans: data corruption, failures that cause the database to be unavailable, and data center disasters that destroy the complete computing environment. Each risk must be described and the mitigation detailed in the agreement, along with any expenses or other expectations negotiated.

Data Corruption

Data corruption happens very rarely these days because of the available advanced storage technology protections and database level checks, but no one can provide a 100% guarantee against corruption occurring. Corruption is a nasty bugger, probably the worst event for DBAs. Coordinating with the DBaaS vendor for recovery must be defined ahead of time, including each party's responsibilities.

Disk–level database replication for disaster recovery protection is great; for corruption, it quickly propagates the problem to the recovery site. Backups may include the corruption if detection was delayed. Point-in-time recovery means data loss, but hopefully not more than SLA-agreed loss.

Although the DBaaS provider may offer solutions, you are ultimately responsible for the recovery. Consider periodic disk snapshots or using a product such as Oracle's Data Guard to have a standby database in place that is protected by block-level integrity checks before the log is applied to the database. Once the corruption is discovered, a cutover to the standby database restores service for your customers.

Failure: DB Down

After recovery, the primary consideration when a DBaaS database crashes is to determine the root cause. Without access to the OS and lower stack, the provider has to perform the root cause analysis. That requirement needs to be included in the arrangement, along with an availability and/or return to service SLA inclusion.

Catastrophic Data Center Event

Even the most well-built data centers are susceptible to disaster, whether natural, accidental, or intentional. Companies spend a lot of money to have a secondary data center that is geographically separated from the primary data center and populated with a large or equal percentage of equipment ready to become the primary data center.

If you are using DBaaS to keep from managing a data center and maintaining infrastructure, you will certainly want to also use DBaaS for disaster recovery. Therefore, ensure that the provider's disaster recovery plan clearly defines the recovery process, and is required to exercise and report on at least an annual disaster recovery test.

Encryption

Data protection, whether required by PCI-DSS, HIPAA, or any of the many other governance controls, becomes more necessary when a DBaaS solution is deployed. DBaaS solutions need to include encryption, which can be a hardware or software solution covering database data and data at rest. Storing and transmitting data outside of the corporate walls increase risk, so protecting all data with encryption is smart.

The DBaaS vendor may offer an encrypted storage solution option that makes implementing encryption much easier. Otherwise, encryption may need to be implemented within the database if it is an option, or a third-party package may work but have performance implications.

Access Control and Auditing

Criminal or accidental access to a database continues to be a huge organizational risk. Likewise, many (too many) governing bodies require audits for various reasons. Auditing may require DBAs to not choose the best database for their needs; instead, they select a good database match that includes auditing, although custom auditing can be built without too much pain. Work with the DBaaS provider to understand auditing controls—remember that it is in the vendors best interest to make sure that your data is protected, including the way violations or intrusions are reported. The provider wants to protect you as much as you want to protect your company.

Leveraging single sign-on provides internal clients access to local and external applications, relieving them from having to remember another password or dealing with two-factor authentication protocols. Build in security with simplicity for your customers.

Data Archiving

Multitiered storage and/or data archiving products help manage aging data, preventing performance and space management problems introduced as the data volume increases. Be sure to consider an archiving solution when working with the DBaaS provider. If the provider can make data archiving easier by offering the right archiving tools, it is probably worth investigating. For data archiving, be sure to define how and where it will be done.

Other Customers' Problem Impact

Experience has taught many of us that a problem with one system within a data center can (and probably will) impact other systems. That same consequence must be addressed for DBaaS environments. If the DBaaS solution you plan to use is offered by a provider that would be considered a co-location provider (having many customers within the same data center), understanding the data center infrastructure is essential. Knowing whether another customer's problem, maybe a rogue batch job sending terabytes of data out of the data center, could potentially harm your applications leads to an exercise showing that this provider does not have enough isolation between customer systems. It matters not to the CEO or the Board that the reason why your customers could not spend money on your products or that the business teams were late closing the monthly financials by 4 hours is because company XYZ's batch job consumed all the network bandwidth. Instead, the feedback may be quite pointed: "You should have known that was a risk and managed it."

Fortunately, data center providers have learned much over the past decades, prompting highly modular data center design solutions. Today, customers may still be considered as co-located—primarily geographical nearness only, but also supported by isolated power, network, telecommunications, and so on. Imagine rows and columns of stacked shipping containers, each with direct and independent power, environment, data and voice transmission networks, and compute and storage, surrounded by a building shell in which the hallways on each floor lead to the container doors for physical access. This data center model is not imaginary; it actually exists in several flavors.

Modular separation greatly diminishes the risk of another customer's issue becoming your own. Translating the data center isolation need to DBaaS separation challenges DBAs. Here, co-location is not a building-level consideration, but instead a compute and storage concern. Providers are leveraging virtual capabilities, which means running many virtual guests on the underlying physical servers. Therefore, many customers could have guest hosts sharing the same physical server on which your database is hosted. Be sure that the database resources assigned to your implementation cannot be "borrowed" by other guests. Virtual systems can be overprovisioned, meaning that guests can "borrow" unused compute and memory resources from other guests. Databases do *not* like having their resources borrowed. Nothing delivers performance degradation faster than having the database cache suddenly forced into swapping due to another guest "borrowing" what was believed to be unused memory. Verify with the vendor that the guest resources can be "locked" to prevent other guests from stealing resources.

Monitoring and Synthetic Transactions

When searching for a DBaaS solution, monitoring and synthetic transactions may be a critical add-on service offering from the provider, which should be leveraged. Too often, companies invest tens of millions of dollars building or acquiring, and implementing and supporting applications and infrastructure, only to chintz out by not investing in the right support tools. Fighter jet designers and engineers include navigation and threat warning systems to help pilots "see" where they are going and to avoid risks. It's perplexing how many IT "pilots" are "flying" blind in the application cockpit, unable to detect business-disrupting threats. Implement great systems *and* implement the tools needed to keep the systems great!

When DBaaS is the best solution for your organization, keeping vigilant becomes imperative. Work with the provider to determine how tools can be implemented, what monitoring the vendor provides, and how you are notified of failures or looming performance degradations. I mention this based on outsourcing experiences in which the outsourcing company did not include monitoring in the bid, and the customer assumed that monitoring was foundational. The miscommunication then came to light in the middle of the night when a major failure occurred. Small details matter, hence my intended inclusion in this book.

As just mentioned, tossing the database into the cloud does not relieve DBAs from oversight responsibility. Does the provider offer a monitoring solution? Will the solution integrate with an existing tool suite? Does the solution include the ability to create and monitor synthetic transactions to baseline and alert threshold variances for critical transactions? DBAs must have performance data visibility.

Performance between the database and the client, whether the client is an application server or a person's workstation, also has to be monitored. If it's reported that the database is causing application slowness, DBAs must be able to identify where the slowness is being introduced. Even if you can prove that the database is responding well, you remain on the hook until the root cause is identified. Many DBAs, myself included, worked to become infrastructure "experts" from necessity because it became a requisite to absolutely prove that the database was not at fault. You have experienced the calls that ask, "Is the database is down/slow?" Even when logic disagrees: 20 people report the database being down (the other 10,000 users are silent), and someone at the help desk escalates to the DBA team and carbon copies the entire IT leadership team that the world is about to implode due to this perceived catastrophe. Even before you get a chance to access the database to try to determine why 20 people could be having a problem—DBAs must always check their own backyard before complaining about someone else's—your bosses' boss is already texting you and asking when the database will be back up. OK, that is a bit extreme because most of my bosses have never been so quick to panic, but you get the idea. DBAs must be able to prove that the database is not the culprit and then work with others to determine the root cause.

Having the right monitoring tools and specific synthetic transactions in play minimizes the time needed to find and correct the problem. Otherwise, consider yourself to be much like a fighter jet pilot without a navigation system who is trying to locate an aircraft carrier in an ocean.

Network Configuration Matters

Whether they are a cloud provider's or your company's, shared environments require us to systematically assess all components to ensure that even at peak demand—every customer using every system at full capacity—the business and its customers are not negatively impacted by degraded performance.

Total network bandwidth (and, more importantly, the way the total is actually amassed) needs to be understood and then matched to predicted traffic patterns. DBaaS via a cloud provider means that data read or written to the database must travel some distance (refer to the earlier latency discussion). Forecasting data usage and architecting the infrastructure and application wisely to allow DBaaS to be leveraged without harming application performance or customer expectations becomes a critical task.

Bandwidth and bandwidth configuration need to be considered for peak load and unexpected load caused by failures or irregular traffic. Because the connection to the DBaaS provider is over some form of WAN, not over a LAN, there may be less bandwidth available to absorb the lost capacity. If your location happens to be geographically close to the provider, a metropolitan area network (MAN) or other form of "wired city" network may provide plenty of bandwidth with little distance-caused latency.

When I was asked to investigate repeated reports of slowness at a small site (about 16 people), I discovered that the site had two 1.54 megabits frame relay connections. One of the connections became saturated almost every day during the lunch window. A quick traffic capture revealed significant streaming video traffic, which turned out to be company-mandated training. The root problem was not that the streaming video caused slowness for the applications because team members were obligated to watch the training; instead, there was a failure to communicate between the training and IT departments. Had the infrastructure been considered, it would have been transparent immediately that the company's smaller sites did not have enough bandwidth to conduct normal operations and watch the mandatory training as streaming video. Other arrangements could have been considered, keeping the business from experiencing a disruption.

Scale that problem into a DBaaS provider's infrastructure with many customers, each reading and writing varied data types. Sufficient bandwidth construction becomes a key performance protector.

A gigabit of bandwidth can be designed either as a single connection or as a combination of several smaller connections. They might seem to be equal, but we know that it's much more complicated than that. Never mind the single point-of-failure because vendors know better; focus instead on the delivery capability of the two solutions. DBAs, although probably not network gurus, can easily translate network configuration into database configuration, knowing that multiple read/write connections to a storage array distributes the load, which results in overall better response times. They can apply the same principles, understanding that thousands of customers who reach out to the database from many locations, doing a mixture of work, can benefit from many I/O (network) paths.

DBaaS and Continuous Integration

Fortunately, DBaaS and CI does not look much different from on-premise database and CI when it comes to database changes. DBAs still need to automate database changes to integrate with application changes, maintain all code in the source code repository, and provide tests to thoroughly vet the changes.

Database template builds and execution may no longer be something DBAs need to manage because the provider probably controls and provides the DBaaS platform.

Summary

Considering DBaaS leads down an exciting and challenging path of leveraging "old school" DBA skills: design, access control, recoverability, scalability, performance, and more; combined with ensuring that the shiny new cloud model does not introduce unacceptable latency, shared database or data center risks, or problems when you are not fully in control of the build configuration.

Costs can be leveled out, changing only as capacity increments or decrements; performance and scalability are easily managed given the virtualization mode; database selection varies so that the best database can be selected, instead of forcing square data into a round database.

Each "as a Service" offering provides IT shops, including DBAs, the prerogative to select the right database for the job. Matching team capabilities to specific technology stack layers encourages smart decisions in which the provider's expertise and the company's expertise meld together for an optimal business operations solution.

Final thought: if DBaaS offerings are too restrictive, going with a PaaS solution provides the opportunity to build databases per your specifications.

Overcoming Language and Cultural Barriers Between DBAs and DevOps

The collaborative foundation of DevOps decrees positive and well-intentioned communications. Defining rules of engagement that satisfy this expectation equips each team member for success. Knowing that communication underlies and perpetuates all aspects of DevOps encourages team members toward effective communications.

IT people—nerds, geeks, techies, or whatever stereotypical or imaginable name you can recall—are very effective communicators, but only when discussing programming, gaming, cryptology, infrastructure, cloud technologies, multiplayer role games, Star Wars versus Star Trek, the existence of

© Michael S. Cuppett 2016
M. S. Cuppett, *DevOps, DBAs, and DBaaS*, DOI 10.1007/978-1-4842-2208-9_10

extraterrestrial life, space and/or time travel, and many other fascinating topics. However, geek communication does not translate beyond the tech world. Yes, I just stereotyped myself and many of you in jest; in my experience, it is not that stereotypical because many of us communicate well beyond the cubicles.

Sadly, the exact same translation problem can impede conversations between DBAs and DevOps team members. Patience and effort together blend taxonomies and process methodologies for the betterment of DevOps. Each entity, DBA, or DevOps team member must take personal responsibility for the success of this talent merger. Years of resentment and uncooperativeness has brought team division to new heights. The cultural position of DevOps brings opportunities to bridge the divide for true team partnerships.

Because DevOps continues to achieve emergent momentum, DBAs might need to come around a bit further than the already engaged DevOps players. As with any movement or incipient technology framework, new nomenclature develops that takes time to learn and understand. Existing DevOps team members need to educate DBAs on terminology as much as practical DevOps techniques and tools.

After becoming familiar with the DevOps approach and pertinent processes and tools, DBAs introduce database practice experience to expand perceptions of data protection, schema management, data transformation, and database build best practices. DBAs who meld database management approaches into DevOps practices that are aligned with shared goals are successful only if the DevOps team members understand DBA methods and can see the value brought to the overall DevOps model.

Rules of Engagement

Guidelines are important for communicating and working effectively because differing collaborative terms pop up every few years with different names and different bullet points. They all have the same purpose: to respect each person and the value he or she offers. As a United States Army veteran, a term such as *rules of engagement* resonates. Aligned with the DevOps principles, here is an easily understandable set of guardrails to keep us all communicating and operating efficiently:

- Goal alignment: Have a collaborative approach among team members who agree on common goals and incentives: strive to harvest excellent software products hosted on sustainable and stable infrastructures while continuously improving processes, automation, and cycle time.

- Deliverable coresponsibility: No single actor should be allowed to dominate or distort the principles, direction, or team accountability and actions, thus safeguarding DevOps guidelines and the Agile self-forming team concept.

- Speak to the outcomes: Require constant and consistent verbal communications for expeditious task coordination and execution, matched by effective and timely decisions to drive expected outcomes.

- Change adaptation: Accept business and customer fluidity as product requirement drivers while slaying traditional project management strategies better guarantees project success.

- Give the benefit of the doubt: Grant people grace, and trust that their intentions are good and intended for the team's benefit. Embrace the possibility that you may be the person causing team tension and then stop doing so.

DevOps Speak

Continuous may be the most frequently heard word in DevOps conversations. Here's why:

Continuous…

- flow: Work is always progressing and driven by automation, having value deliberately built in at a sustainable pace. Several Agile methods specifically limit the amount of work that can be in process at the same time. Limiting work-in-progress grants focus and time to properly construct the product and product testing, which lead to better outcomes without overpressuring the staff.

- build: Build tests and code, preferably in that order. With QA shifting to the development stage, code with fewer defects can be created at lower total cost of ownership.

- integration: Combine new or changed application code with the core product through extensive functional and performance testing, and correct defects immediately to produce the next product version.

- delivery: Ensure that the software product is positioned at all times for production release or deployment, encapsulating the building, testing, and integration processes.

Successful integration produces the deliverable, making continuous delivery a product state, not a process.

- deployment: Where applicable, production deployments should occur as soon as the product is ready for release after integration (this is less likely for legacy environments).

- feedback: There should be persistent communications concerning the product quality, performance, and functionality intending to find, report, and fix bugs faster or to correct performance earlier in the pipeline. Commit to the "shift-left" concept.

- improvement: Apply lean principles to eliminate waste, build in value, reduce defects, and shorten cycle time to improve product quality. Team members should take time to reflect on completed projects or sprints to increase productivity by staking claim to value-adding tasks and shedding inefficiencies and unproductive steps.

Depending on the tools used, product themes abound. There are chefs with recipes, cookbooks, kitchens, and supermarkets; a butler, puppets, blowfish, broccoli, maven, ant, and many other strange yet fun product names. Check out XebiaLabs' Periodic Table of DevOps Tools.

Automation and Orchestration

Automation focuses on executing tasks quickly. Building a script to run a set of database change commands is automation. *Orchestration* focuses on process or work flow. Building a series of steps to execute tasks in a defined order to produce an outcome is orchestration.

Spinning up a virtual database host combines automation (the set of commands for each task) and orchestration to run the tasks logically.

DBA "Speak"

Languages vary among DBAs. For example, application DBAs talk code execution efficiency, logical DBAs (aka data architects) talk about normal forms, and operational DBAs talk about performance. DBAs also know plenty of ways to skin a cat. *No animals were harmed in the making of this book.* Yet DBAs manage to keep databases humming along—most of the time. Although there are differences in DBA roles and responsibilities, the end game is database stability, performance, availability, security, and recoverability (to name just a handful). DevOps team members must understand the DBAs' database protectiveness and self-preservation tendencies. After spending long nights and weekends recovering from code deployments that took months to build and test, it makes less sense on the surface to reduce the time spent building and testing the software.

DevOps team members are challenged to shine a light on the new paradigm and emphasize that the speed is offset by fewer code changes, which improves the odds for a successful deployment. Also let the DBAs know that as a DevOps team, failures cause all team members—including developers—to be all hands on deck. Now that it is in everyone's best interest to implement change correctly, DBAs are no longer the only people pursuing self-preservation.

Language and Culture: More than the Spoken Tongue and Traditions

The IT world is diverse on many levels, which is great! I have learned much from working with people in the United States, but also in South Korea, West Germany (I still make the distinction because I was serving in West Germany when the Berlin Wall fell), and for about a week in Brazil. I have also learned things from people in other states because diversity is needed.

As DBAs and DevOps team members come together, the differences add the value. Think about it; if everyone on the team knows the same things, all but a single person are redundant. People speaking different languages figure out how to communicate effectively, so DBAs and DevOps team members can do the same. The difference is often perspective, which I have mentioned before: repetition reinforces ideas. DevOps is more a cultural shift for IT than a process shift. Sure, the tools and schedules are different, but those elements are easy to learn or adapt to; a culture shift requires time to digest the idea and bring everyone along.

Let's take a look at the world of IT from different perspectives to begin to understand where DevOps is taking us all.

Resiliency versus Complexity

Resiliency describes the ability to sustain operations or to quickly restore operations when failure occurs. For application systems with data stores, database clustering provides resiliency—the failure of one node does not reduce transactional throughput. That happens when the cluster is built to withstand a single node failure, with the remaining nodes sized to maintain 100% capacity at mandated response times. A pool of web or application servers distributes the workload while improving resiliency because surviving nodes maintain operations when a node fails.

Resiliency can be scaled to meet financial considerations. Under the plan using the clustered database example, a single node loss could result in a 30% decrease in load capacity; mitigation must be preplanned to stop or deprioritize enough load to not impact critical operations. For example, batch processing or reporting can be suspended until the system is at full capacity.

DevOps provides an answer to the capacity problem if the database clustering can benefit from the host build template scripts. The loss of one node can be quickly offset by an automated build of a new node that can be introduced into the cluster. Furthermore, additional capacity can be activated when demand exceeds capability.

Resiliency from clustering and other high-availability solutions does have a drawback: *complexity*. Be sure to not increase complexity to an unsustainable level when designing critical systems. Overly complex systems with tricky interdependencies that create situations in which maintenance and upgrades are postponed defeats the purpose of resiliency. Being resilient requires keeping pace with database upgrades and security patching to increase stability and prevent breaches or data theft.

Rolling upgrades and patches signal resiliency by demonstrating the capability to maintain continuous operations while simultaneously improving the platform. Extending this capability to be able to completely replace the database environment with an upgraded or different database altogether, and with a fallback plan in place to return to the previous platform, exemplifies resiliency.

DevOps brings about the opportunity to maintain resiliency with less complexity because web, app, or database servers can be built in minutes or hours instead of the weeks or months it used to take to acquire and build servers. Virtualization is a major enabler of DevOps.

Building Simplicity

Simplifying architecture and application code runs counterintuitive to real–life IT solutions design, yet it is still a smart move for the long run. True solutions design not only leads to the best possible product but it also restrains from adding anything distracting to the product. As DBAs and DevOps team members unite, they resolve to fight complexity with design eloquence and minimalist tendencies, and prevent complexity from entangling DBA processes that may harm pipeline efficiency. Excitement builds as expectations for simple, precise, and demonstratively improved business systems are realized from this joining of forces.

Packaging and Propagation

Thoughtful and well-planned database software build packaging and propagation can be used to maintain resiliency, as described previously, but it can also be used for on-demand capacity, multisite distributive processing, and maintenance of pipeline database consistency. Packaging versioned releases for upgrade simplification must include database owner and other account privileges needed for distribution. Database installs in which an OS hook must be executed by an administrator account need to be scripted to pull needed credentials during execution. The scripting must also ensure that password information does not get written to the installation or audit logs.

The shift goes from lengthy and tedious manual installs or lightly automated installs to a completely automated build that can be done fast enough that IT has the agility to immediately respond to demand, not after weeks of struggling to keep a system running in overload mode.

Structured and Unstructured

For decades, the relational database has been the database of choice, and large companies have invested millions in licensing and platforms. Without viable options, project data storage requirements landed in a relational database management system (RDBMS), regardless of the data structure or even the content. More recently, many newer, viable database options are becoming mainstream, but it is still a hard sell to convince the upper echelon that additional investment is needed for another database ecosystem. Even open-source databases come with staff support and hardware costs, or monthly DBaaS payments. Forcing data models into unsuitable databases deoptimizes solutions. From the start, performance is less than it could be than when a better–fitting database engine manages the data.

Maturing DevOps organizations lean toward optimized solutions, making force-feeding data into a database unthinkable. Relational databases remain "top dogs" as databases of record for transactional data. As applications shift toward multiple database back ends, services or APIs provide data call abstraction to maintain flow.

Unicorn companies start with very little cash flow, limiting the affordable scope of databases. Open-source databases enable individuals and small teams to build application software with a data store. As these companies grew, the databases scaled to the point at which other companies took notice. When CIOs drive down IT costs, looking at alternative databases becomes a viable (and street-proven) option. DevOps leverages this learning, making it possible to store data in the database best suited for the content, pulling along cost-cutting options.

Audit Trail

Audit reviews are a necessity when build automation replaces human control. DBAs who install software pay attention to the screen messages, responding to configuration questions and noting errors that need attention. The risk is that the same person might do a second install that is not exactly like the first. Vendors have included automation scripts for years, but platform differences still happen. DevOps automation is meant to build the complete platform without a person making decisions because the decisions are built in to the automation or gathered before automation execution.

A developer requesting a new web server should need to provide only primitive inputs up front—OS, web server brand, and a few sizing parameters—before the automation kicks off. There are legitimate reasons to pause automation, but asking for more information should not be one of them. As mentioned, automation is task based, so stopping the orchestration is more likely. The automation and orchestration need to generate audit trails.

True to DevOps, audit log checkout should be automated because no DBA or DevOps team member wants to review pages and pages of audit information. Learning which error codes or other failures to search for tightens the noose around inconsistency. More importantly, governing bodies require documentation for application changes, which makes the audit log that evidence.

Repeatability

Repeatability of tests or builds improves the efficiency of code, and infrastructure as code, along the full continuous delivery pipeline. Being able to build servers quickly allows developers to experiment with different code techniques or operations to build capacity on demand. DBAs are used to being responsible for database builds, so it may take a little time for them to get used to the idea of developers building and destroying databases at will.

DBAs can instead create templates for the way databases are built, which seems like a better deal. Limiting the numbers of unique database software installs and database builds has advantages. Code should execute exactly the same within a version. Troubleshooting narrows from having fewer possible variables. Once a problem is found, knowing where to apply the fix is easy. When testing a change, the way the database executes with the change should be consistent on like architectures. As much as possible, the nonproduction environment should mirror production, decreasing the chance of change failure caused by underlying configuration differences.

Build repeatability is a win for developers, DBAs, and DevOps team members.

Security

Nothing causes a puckering posture more than a potential data breach. On the scale of security threat mitigation, preventing data breaches sits at or near the top. Partnering with the information security team, DBAs play an inherent role in data protection. DBAs, as custodians of the corporate data assets, consider security a key deliverable.

Although database access comes in many forms, in all cases access should be granted only after authentication, and each access needs to meet audit requirements. Authentication can be granted by the database, application, or single sign-on protocol. Each authentication must be logged for auditing. Each access, whether as a user request, job initiation, or integration interface, should be uniquely identifiable for auditing. How the auditing is performed is less important than the auditing being done. The auditing may be controlled within the database by using a built-in feature or with application code that writes the audit information to a table or file. Importantly, DBAs should not be able to alter the data once the audit record is created, which protects the information from less-scrupulous DBAs.

Data encryption protects data at rest, including data stored in the database or stored as files. Many database products offer encryption, though it may be easier to use storage-based encryption, which covers the database and file data. At a minimum, Social Security numbers (SSNs), credit card numbers, personal health information, and other sensitive data elements must be protected, which should already be done where compliance with governance requirements such as SOX, HIPAA, PCI-DSS, and more are enforced and audited.

Secure SSL protects data in transit, to and from the database to the application tier or end-user device. Preventing "on the wire" breaches is nearly impossible, but at least it should be challenging for the data to be interpreted.

Developers do consider security and at times write code to implement data protection or data hiding; for example, not allowing application users to see full SSNs (just the last four digits) when the user's role does not require knowing the full SSN. Developers may also code in calls to encryption functions or packages to obfuscate data elements. Storage encryption solutions are usually easier to manage and provide full data coverage, but not all organizations scale to the level at which the cost can be justified.

DevOps automation and orchestration should include security implementations. Configuring SSL and installing certificates should be automated. Creating service accounts needed for application access to the database should be automated. Disabling FTP and Telnet on the host should be automated. Each of these automation pieces are collected for orchestration.

Performance

Computers continue to increase in processing power (more importantly, in transactional throughput), which allows more work to be done in less time. No matter how fast computers become, overhead work always reduces the optimal ceiling. Work minimization improves optimization. Lean methodologies drive out unnecessary work to improve process times and reduce waste and cost. IT shops are learning from lean methodologies, DevOps being one representative model.

Execution plans define how the database engine decides to retrieve, sort, and present the requested information or how to modify the data per instruction. Optimizers do a terrific job building execution plans, although misses still occur. If a query is performing poorly, the execution plan should be an early check in the troubleshooting process. DBAs must interrogate the execution plan to determine appropriateness, which requires experience. Developers make great partners when checking execution plans; they are capable of interpreting the plan in light of what the code was built to do.

Code consistency matters for some database engine implementations. During the process of building execution plans, these databases interpret uppercase and lowercase letters as different, making a simple one-character difference appear to be a completely different statement. Keeping code consistent increases the reusability of plans already stored in the cache. Using replaceable variables may also help optimize cached statement use. As DBAs integrate into DevOps teams, ensuring that solid code practices are in place to ease the database load is a step in the right direction.

"Hidden" predicates can make evaluating code and execution plans more challenging; just consider the possibility when the execution plan seems reasonable while performance lags. Security implementations may be the culprit, and one might expect the "secrets" to not be revealed. An easy test to determine whether hidden predicates used by Oracle's Virtual Private Database (VPD) are in play is simply to run the statement using an account with more authority. Improved performance indicates the need to check for additional predicates. You may have to use a tool from a performance products vendor to find the predicates. Once discovered, improving performance may be as easy as elevating account privileges or executing with an account with more authority. Sometimes reworking the code does not lead to enough performance improvement, making the privileges decision the fix. Also, if you know that something like VPD is implemented; jobs and reports suddenly take a dive in performance by two-, three-, or four-fold (or more); and the database was not changed, check account security because it is not beyond the realm of possibility that a security job was run to correct perceived audit discrepancies.

Optimized code sheds unneeded work and data touches (the latter is critical to result set size) and reporting and ETL processes in the context of batch.

Selective predicates—the where clause statements—reduce execution effort and time while also lessening the burden on the database as a whole. DBAs understand, and developers and DevOps team members need to learn, that each segment of work contributes to the overall database load. Therefore, anything that can be done to reduce work at the statement level benefits all database transactions.

Leverage indexes for improved performance. Performance drags when large data scans are performed unnecessarily, making index selection critical. Whether an index was not considered as the code was built and implemented, or the statement was written so the optimizer decided that no existing index met the execution needs, performance suffers. Today's computing power and high-performing database engines contribute to response times in the low milliseconds for simple transactional reads and writes, meaning that DBAs should seriously question response times that take a second or longer.

Kernel configuration undergirds databases and applications, ensuring resource availability. DBAs who lack kernel-tuning experiences are missing an opportunity to truly take full advantage of the underlying hardware and OS. DBaaS solutions being preconfigured leaves kernel configuration and tuning in the hands of the provider. Otherwise, DBAs should work in tandem with SAs to monitor and tweak the kernel for better performance or go with a PaaS solution for more control over the database configuration, at the cost of increased maintenance overhead.

Network configuration is usually not a high-priority performance differentiator; it becomes a concern only when huge data sets have to be transferred over the network. Even then, the primary focus is outside of the databases, requiring OS and/or network configuration tuning. Common modifications include increasing the maximum transmission unit (MTU) to pack more data into each network packet, or (when available) using "jumbo" packets that are dependent on platform options. Either way, the change needs to be done at both endpoints.

Data movement impacts performance based on volume. Remember that networks cannot get faster, only bigger. They are capable of moving more data at the same speed, but the amount of data that needs to be moved directly impacts the time needed for the move. The larger data sets tend to be between the database and the application servers. Latency increases as distance between point A and B increases, extending the time needed to move the data. An easy test: place one application server in the data center that hosts the database and another application server in a location geographically distanced from the database location. Test data pulls of increasing size until the data move duration becomes apparent. Then consider that impact spread across thousands of customers. Even if distance is not a concern, it remains a wise decision to limit the data volume because client machines possess varying network–traffic processing capabilities.

Virtualization has improved server resource usage and facilitated data center consolidation from increased compute density per floor tile. DBAs need to ensure that the assigned virtual resources are "locked" so other guests cannot "steal" resources. Resource reallocation generally helps to balance loads, and it produces excellent results in most cases. Databases are one exception because they do not play well with other kids in the same sandbox. Just for fun, test the scenario in which a guest steals memory from the database guest. Nothing says "horrendous performance" faster than the database cache being swapped in and out of memory!

Teaching

Being able to transfer information in your head to someone else's head should be a required skill for all team members because one Agile precept (extended to DevOps) states that each team member should be able to perform all the team's functions. For DBAs, that implies that you are unlikely to be the only person creating automated database change scripts. Instead, you could be reviewing code and looking at audit files to improve automation execution. Your DevOps teammates have the responsibility of making you a full-fledged team member. On the flipside, DBAs must teach DevOps team members how to manage database changes to support the development pipeline. This knowledge sharing is a great thing, especially if you want to ever take an uninterrupted vacation.

Teaching can and should be done formally and informally. Formal teaching requires planning, topic definition, and preparation to ensure that the information to be conveyed happens successfully. Informal teaching can be done by sitting next to a team member (similar to extreme programming paired programming) and working through a database change or writing an automation script. Informal teaching includes talking with teammates while having lunch together or when gathered at the team's favorite after-work watering hole.

Sharing knowledge within teams is step 1. Self-forming teams are a key Agile and DevOps element, but self-forming teams do not imply forever teams. As products and demands change, teams eventually disperse and re-form differently, ready to complete new work. Team redistribution leads to knowledge distribution. Something you taught to one team can now be shared within other teams, extending your impact and making teams more effective, while expanding the organizational knowledge base.

Personal development should not be replaced by team training; instead, personal development should inject fresh ideas and skills. Too often, people attend training specific only to their primary technology skill: Java programmers take an advanced Java class, or DBAs take a backup and recovery class for the database platform they support. My approach has always considered three perspectives that I believe fit the DevOps model of shared work.

Tridirectional Training

Core technology or skill: deepening your core skill and intending to become an "expert."

Aligned technology or skill: expanding your sphere of impact by adding complementary skills such as surrounding technologies. General or soft skills: communications, leadership, time management, and business understanding.

Operationalization

After the code has been implemented, the final step in the pre-DevOps model is usually Operations team members figuring out how to implement backups, monitoring, batch processing, reporting, and more. DevOps makes it feasible to gather the operational information earlier in the process, which allows automation to handle much of the operationalization. For example:

- Backups: Backup software or agents can be installed and configured during the server build, including setting the schedule.

- Monitoring: Like backups, software or agents can be installed and configured, and registered to the administrative or master console, including baseline performance settings.

- Scheduling batch and report jobs: Load management pertains to distributing background work across the day interval to not impact transactional systems while completing batch and report work. Scheduling can be automated, even with load protections to delay execution for a prescribed time if the system load is high.

- Capacity management: Not the annual growth predications, but real-time activity, monitoring provides opportunities to take proactive steps to add capacity on demand, or at least to plan for capacity to be added soon. Adding a fifth application server in real time to a four-node app server farm quickly provides 25% more capacity, provided you have the needed server build automation in place. Once the server is built and ready for traffic, a quick update to the load balancer can be made to start directing traffic to the expansion server. Imagine being able to upgrade the entire farm by building replacement servers with higher transaction throughput and then making changes at the load balancer to insert the new servers and delete the old servers. DevOps automation opens new windows to improve operational performance and resiliency with real-time capacity management. Capacity management needs to consider more than database growth; instead it should encompass the full IT supply chain, up- and downstream.

Availability

Resiliency is the capability of a system to continue to function or recover quickly from failure. Being designed and baked into an application architecture that results in a high-availability infrastructure implementation able to tolerate single device failures affords strong continuous business capability. A three-node server cluster built with enough horsepower that a single node failure can be absorbed by the two remaining servers without performance degradation demonstrates resiliency.

Failover is a methodology for moving a failed or significantly impaired production environment onto another similar system, usually located near or in close proximity to the primary system. One caution comes in the form of the statement "failover to DR," which may not mean exactly what is stated.

Cost and complexity decisions weighed against business needs may lead to investments in like systems or smaller investments to provide a portion of the transactional capability of the primary systems as a stopgap until the main production platform can be operationally restored. The transition involves redirecting all computers communicating to the failed system, which may simply be updating a few entries in a load balancer or be a complicated and tedious effort to manually point each interfacing system to the temporary production environment, having to repeat the same effort to fall back to normal operations.

Recoverability

Recovery dictates backup requirements. Many DBAs ask, "How should I back up an X TB database?" The question should actually be this: "How should I back up an X TB database when the business demands a 2-hour recovery window?" Understand that the recovery requirements drives the backup solution. With DBaaS, the recovery requirement needs to be settled as a deliverable in the SLA. An in-house backup may be to disk or to a virtual tape solution (disk) that is capable of recovering an X TB database in under 2 hours. Because the business wants the recovery to take no longer than 2 hours, the recovery must allow time to start the database and reconnect dependent systems before access is granted.

Server failures without the aforementioned resiliency models in place to maintain operations are more complicated to recover. The whole system may have be to be recovered from backup, or with DevOps automation the host environment could be rebuilt new from a template package, followed by the database restore.

Disaster recovery is a program designed to protect the business from a catastrophic failure, most likely the destruction of a data center. This form of recovery must be specifically planned and exercised, with predetermined executives authorized to declare the event and open the checkbook to cover the costs of people, vendors, and computing resources needed to recover automated business operations in a geographically distanced data center. DRaaS options are relatively new, albeit gaining respect and maturing quickly.

Business continuity is the business-side recovery process when disaster strikes, including an event requiring the disaster recovery program to be activated. Business continuity is more likely to be activated due to a natural disaster or civil unrest than failure of the company's data center. Planning and exercising options lead to success. Knowing how to operate the business during crisis—civil, natural disaster, or technology unavailability—covers a much broader scope than the disaster recovery program.

DevOps automation, mentioned briefly here, brings a new and exciting option to the world of recovery. The capability to generate new virtual hosts or full application host environments on demand quickly presents the opportunity to improve recovery times. Database hosts can be rebuilt, but the database must be recovered. More apparently, web and application servers built from predefined templates and install packages should be considered and tested for recovery-time comparison. Having the ability to build systems quickly as a recovery process frees traditional resources for other work. If the current disaster recovery program includes replication between the primary and DR site, consider stopping the replication of web and app servers; for example, instead opt to build these servers on demand, potentially saving bandwidth costs. Ensure that the DR location has available resources for the automated build restores.

Summary

DevOps is opportunity. Bringing together talented professionals to complete new missions by using new methods and tools facilitates business agility and growth while improving customer experience and developing IT team members. Two obstacles—language and culture—can be easily overcome with frequent communication, the willingness to share experiences, and selfless knowledge sharing. The end game is to build great DevOps teams that are capable of delivery software and infrastructure better and faster than ever.

Adding DBAs to DevOps teams amps up team capabilities while making it possible to reduce risk by incorporating database builds, configurations, and changes into the Agile pipeline. This addition also removes a long sidelined process outlier to just another automation to be included in the orchestration.

Index

A

Application performance
    management (APM), 7

Automation and code control
    auditable, 119
    automating out errors, 114–115
    bare bones disaster recovery, 120
    benefits, 110–111
    Chaos management, 119
    check-in snowballs, 118
    code control, 118
    conflicting interests, 110
    continuous delivery, 118
    Craftsmanship, 108
    human vs. computer, 108
    leaner model, 109–110
    no value-add work, 109
    orchestration, 116
    performance, 117
    release cycle shrink
        distinct units of work, 114
        parallelism, 113–114
        testing, 111–112
    roll back/roll over, 119
    tribal knowledge, 121
    workarounds, 116
    zero defects!, 115

AVERAGE() function, 67–68

B

Browser's Inspect tool, 79

Buffer cache thrashing, 17–18

Business analyst (BA), 3

C

Canary releases, 30

Change advisory board (CAB), 15–16

Chef tool, 54

Code abstraction, 61–62

Containerization, 35

Continuous delivery (CD), 6, 118

Continuous integration, 21

Continuous loopback system, 11

Continuous testing, 21

Couchbase, 53

Create Index statement, 84

Culture, automation, measurement,
    sharing (CAMS), 7–11

Cumulative degradation, 6–7

D, E

Dark release, 33

Database administrators (DBAs).
        See also DevOps
    bridg-ers
        collaboration and automation, 16
        continuous integration, 21
        continuous testing, 21
        customer delight, 19
        "fail fast, fail forward" model, 20
        processes, 19
        reciprocal teaching, 17–18
        tools of trade, 22
        transition, 16–17

Database administrators (DBAs) (*cont.*)
    CAB, 15
    integration (see Integrating process)
    language and cultural barriers (see
        Language and cultural barriers)
    molding, 23
    value proposition, 23

Database as a Service (DBaaS), 3
    access control and auditing, 133
    APIs/services methods, 130
    architecture
        configuration inflexibility, 131
        latency, 130
    company's data repositories, 130
    continuous integration, 137
    customers' problem impact, 134
    for DevOps, 130
    encryption, 133
    implementation, 129
    monitoring and synthetic
        transactions, 135
    multitiered storage and data
        archiving products, 134
    network configuration matters, 136
    recoverability
        catastrophic data center event, 133
        data corruption, 132
        failures, 132
    scalability, 131

Database technology integration
    change failures, 51–52
    nonrelational databases, 52–53, 56
    resources
        build information, 47
        log file, 47–48
        platform readiness, 45
        prerequisites, 46
        virtualization, 45
    rotating toward development, 42–44
    source code control
        application and database code, 48
        availability, 49
        CI process, 49
        database changes, 50
        metadata changes, 49
    tools, 54–55
data testing, 38

DevOps
    automated testing, 6
    business analyst, 3
    CAMS, 7–11
    continuous delivery, 6
    continuous integration, 6
    customer experience performance
        protectors, 6–7
    database selection, 4
    infrastructure enablers, 3–4
    integrating process
        (see Integrating process)
    language and cultural barriers (see
        Language and cultural barriers)
    nonproduction and production
        environments, 13
    quality assurance, 1–2
    SDLC, 11–12
    security, 12
    sharing performance metrics, 5
    Shift-left illustration, 2
    technical advisors, 4–5

Disaster Recovery as a
    Service (DRaaS), 105

F, G

Fail fast, fail forward model, 20

H

HttpWatch browser proxy capture, 78

I

Input measurement, DBA
    core application, with extensive
        integration dependencies, 91
    customer experience, 88–89
    DevOps and virtualization, 89
    direct DBA impact
        application code, 101
        code reuse, 102
        database, 99
        minimal data touch, 102
        operating system, 99
        result set, 102
        storage system, 100
    holistic end-user experience, 90

online retailers design infrastructure and
   applications, 88
optimal
   application ecosystem, 96
   costs, 97
   cumulative degradation, 95
   foundational/simple troubleshooting
      techniques, 96
   manufacturing process, 94
   NIC, 96
   RRPs/IRP, 97
peripheral DBA influence
   capacity, 104
   DRaaS, 105
   end-user devices, 104
   network, 103
   recoverability, 105
pragmatic, 97
proximity matters, 98
real-time application monitoring, 92
scenarios, 89
transaction time, 93

Integrating processes, 5
   canary releases, 30–31
   code handling pre-and
      postdatabase change, 28–29
   containerization, 35
   dark release, 33
   database changes, 26
   database release, 34
   data testing, 38
   DB/App releases, 27
   disruptive release, 26
   disruptors, 26
   landscape evolution, 34
   manual to automatic process, 36
   microservices, 34
   node migration, 32–33
   performance testing, 36–38
   release considerations, 29
   rolling upgrades, 32
   template integration, 36

Incident response plans (IRPs), 97

Infrastructure as a Service (IaaS), 126

J, K

Java virtual machines (JVMs), 35

Jenkins tool, 54

L

Landscape evolution, 34

Language and cultural barriers
   audit trail, 146
   automation, 142
   availability, 152
   delivery, 141
   deployment, 142
   engagement rules, 140
   feedback, 142
   flow, 141
   improvement, 142
   integration, 141
   operationalization
      backup software or agents, 151
      capacity management, 151
      monitoring, 151
      scheduling batch and
         report jobs, 151
   orchestration, 142
   packaging and propagation, 145
   performance
      code consistency matters, 148
      code optimization, 148
      data movement impacts, 149
      execution plans, 148
      kernel configuration, 149
      leverage indexes, 149
      network configuration, 149
      teaching, 150
      virtualization, 150
      VPD, 148
   recoverability, 152
   repeatability, 146
   resiliency *vs.* complexity, 143
   security, 147
   speak, 142
   structured and unstructured, 145
   tongue and traditions, 143
   tridirectional training, 151

Legacy production environment, 37

M

Maximum transmission
      unit (MTU), 149

Microservices, 34

MongoDB database, 52, 63

N

Neo4j, 53–54

Network interface card (NIC), 96

Node migration, 32–33

Nonrelational databases, 52–53

O

Operationalization
  backup software/agents, 151
  capacity management, 151
  monitoring, 151
  scheduling batch and report jobs, 151

Optimizing application performance
  binary indicator, 74
  call center representatives, 75
  code distribution, 76
  customer-centric statuses, 82
  deployments, 81
  excessive testing vets, 81
  infrastructure, 75
  ITIL ITSM process, 73
  melding application performance, 74
  packet capture tool, 80
  performance isolation
    business-empowering function, 85
    CI testing, 85
    Create Index statement, 84
    customer experience, 85
    MongoDB database, 84
    time-consuming, 85
    transaction breakpoints, 83
    WAN segment, 84
  repeatable tasks, 81
  repetitive code testing, 81
  shift-left and work, 81
  user–reported application
    end-to-end response time, 77–80
    objective timings, 77

Oracle's Virtual Private Database (VPD), 148

P

Performance testing, 36–38

Platform as a Service (PaaS), 127

Q

Quality assurance (QA), 1–2

R

Rapid response plans (RRPs), 97

Reciprocal teaching, 17–18

Recovery point objective (RPO), 105

Recovery time objective (RTO), 105

Relational database management
    system (RDBMS), 145

S

Sharing performance metrics, 6

Software as a Service (SaaS)
  "as a Service" offerings, 126
  "as a Service" products, 126
  ecosystem, 124

Software development life
    cycle (SDLC), 1, 2, 4, 5,
    10–12, 19, 22, 42, 110, 112

Source code control, 36
  application and database code, 48
  availability, 49
  CI process, 49
  database changes, 50
  metadata changes, 49

Stateful and stateless programming
  API/microservices, 58
  code abstraction, 61–62
  coding, 67–70
  database schema, 64–67
  data integrity, 61
  definition, 57
  functional data requirements, 60
  live implementations, 59
  NoSQL database, 61
  NoSQL query, 64
  redefining availability, 59–60
  SQL query, 63, 70
  TCP, 58
  UDP, 58
  web page, 71

T

TeamCity tool, 55

Template integration, 36

Template versioning, 36

Transmission Control Protocol (TCP), 58

U, V, W, X, Y, Z

User Datagram Protocol (UDP), 58

User interface (UI), 112

Utility computing. See Infrastructure as a Service (IaaS)

Get the eBook for only $4.99!

Why limit yourself?

Now you can take the weightless companion with you wherever you go and access your content on your PC, phone, tablet, or reader.

Since you've purchased this print book, we are happy to offer you the eBook for just $4.99.

Convenient and fully searchable, the PDF version enables you to easily find and copy code—or perform examples by quickly toggling between instructions and applications.

To learn more, go to http://www.apress.com/us/shop/companion or contact support@apress.com.

Printed in the United States
By Bookmasters